COMPOSING VOICES

A Cycle of Dramatic Monologues

COMPOSING VOICES

A Cycle of Dramatic Monologues

Robert Pack

LOST HORSE PRESS

SANDPOINT & HOPE · IDAHO

ACKNOWLEDGMENTS

The poems collected here were first published in:

The Agni Review, Antaeus, The American Scholar, Black Warrior Review, The Chowder Review, The Denver Quarterly, The Georgia Review, The Gramercy Review, The Hudson Review, The Kenyon Review, The Massachusetts Review, The New England Review, The New Republic, Ploughshares, Poetry Magazine, Poetry Miscellany, Poetry Northwest, Poetry Now, Prairie Schooner, The Seattle Review, The Sewanee Review, The Southern Review, Tendrill Magazine, The Virginia Quarterly.

Some of the poems have been published by David R. Godine in *Faces in a Single Tree* and by The University of Chicago Press in *Fathering the Map.*

The American Scholar awarded the poem, "Prayer for Prayer," The Mary Elinor Smith Poetry Prize.

Book design by Christine Holbert

LIBRARY OF CONGRESS
CATALOGING-IN-PUBLICATION DATA

Pack, Robert, 1929-
Composing voices: a cycle of dramatic monologues / Robert Pack.—
1st ed.
        p. cm.
ISBN 0-9762114-0-8 (alk. paper)
1. Dramatic monologues. I. Title.
PS3566.A28C66 2005
812'.54—dc22
                        2005016316

TABLE OF CONTENTS

I

For John Glendening
. . . in dialogue

Perhaps I can convince you that I am
quite like the other characters you'll meet
within this book—although I have a life
that's more than words where we, alas,
Dear Reader, cannot touch, here in this country
where bright orchestrated words are all
the measured air we can accommodate.
    And so, hail noted Maestro-Muse, inspire
my poems with characters conceivable
to me through whom I can augment my life,
proclaiming an enlarged identity,
my iamb that iamb, pontificating
that I can, while on my beat, encompass
opposites—female and male, happy,
despairing, celebrating, or in grief,
deluded and deluding, sometimes both,
as both are changed and interchanged and then
are interchanged again as I become
someone defined by others who in turn
are seen and changed by me. Not in a void,
or floating in a disembodied mind,
but somewhere set in place and time must all
exchanges between partial selves occur—
as in a room with an embroidered quilt
with intersecting red and yellow squares,
a pear-shaped lamp, a window looking west
out to a lake where coasting ducks suggest
serenity, a couple reconciles
or else prepares to separate,
a daughter tells her mother that she does
not know who is the father of her child
or she's ecstatic with her pregnancy.

More selves arrive within whose lives I lose
and find myself: a father with his hand
upon the shoulder of his son, a mother who
adjusts the scarf around her daughter's throat
as in a snow-smoothed field a cardinal
surveys the desolation of the scene—
a scene which helps prolong my somber mood.
Through all the characters appearing in
the shifting landscapes of their whirling lives,
I see myself in shadows and in shades,
in blue transitions of reflected sky,
perhaps beside a stream, perhaps along
the border of a scented clover field,
whoever at that moment I may be,
but still becoming who I am. I'm here,
emerging in the surge of evening light
or fading but for fictive memory—
distinct as laughter or as sobbing from
a neighbor room or from among dense trees—
here at the flaring edge of startled dawn,
composed in sweet Mozartian delight,
complete, and yet preparing to move on.

THE MARRIAGE MOOSE

Yes, I'm prepared to vow tomorrow on
our wedding day to cherish you until
I die, but wouldn't it, my dear, be much
more realistic if I only claim,
based on the uptodate statistics, that
I will be faithful until some more youthful
damsel should one balmy day come strolling by?
Kidding—of course I'm only kidding—but
we can't control the future, we can't know
what motives drive somebody else's mind
no less our own. And yet I do believe
choice also can affect our destiny,
though not so much perhaps as accident.

Pure chance is what inspired me to propose:
Surely you must recall, the two of us,
only a month or so after we'd met,
were hiking through the woods in Maine,
when suddenly a giant moose appeared
out from behind a stand of hemlock trees,
confronting us, lowering his antlers,
pawing the mush of moss and mashed-down leaves,
rolling his head with widened, glaring eyes.

While clinging to each other, all we thought
to do was hide behind a tangled shrub
enveloped in the shade. Bone-shocking fear
was what we shared that day; nothing was said
and there was nothing else we could have done
but hope the snorting moose would not attack.
Could his moose-mind have speculated we,
entangled in each other's arms, were one—
a creature he had never seen before
and best be wary of? That anxious night
beside the fire when, impassioned, I

proposed to you without considering
how we'd support ourselves or what I'd do
as my life's work, something compelled me then—
and it was not just ordinary lust,
although, God knows, hot blood throbbed in my veins—
to want to make love permanent. Maybe
fear was a part of it, visceral fear
of transience, fear of our fragility
evoked by that encroaching moose. That moose,
that drooling moose, became my Muse incarnate,
thus inspiring in me promises
of loyalty with which I filled the air
in that reverberating forest night.

      Transfigured in my moonlit memory,
antlers diffused into a halo, eyes
set in a constellation of new stars,
the moose in misty spirit will attend
our ceremony of exchanging vows,
proclaiming Love's true triumph over time!

      And so, beyond dull reason, and beyond
what all the world's statistics say, I pledge
fidelity in light of an idea,
a lunatic idea of permanence,
as when, beside a fire ringed with stones,
recounting what we had not counted on—
a story to take with us on our way—
we offered up our thanks for help divine:
our blessed encounter with one baffled moose.

FORTY YEARS LATER

    Dusting the mantelpiece, I carelessly
knocked down the moose you carved to celebrate
the day when, after being chased, still trembling
with the fear of him, we fell in love
so many married years ago. The wood
is brittle dry by now; it broke apart,
its antlers separating from its head.
    I know how proud you are of it, although,
admit! it's not a major work of art.
Without its antlers, the expression on
its droopy face seems kind of farcical;
I think it is beyond repair, though maybe
you can fix it with some glue. You might
decide to keep it for its puzzled look
just as it is. Of course, I'm teasing you!
    I well remember how we hid behind
a rotted stump, assuming he would charge—
the day that you proposed. I think shared fear
gave you the courage to repeat the vows
all lovers feel they have to make. Surely
the harvest moonlight helped, the campfire's warmth,
its swirling sparks like local stars. The past
returns as memory ignites lost passions
I'd forgotten until now—as if the moose
had found a way to both bring back and mock
the raptures we so gladly built upon,
now that acceptance must replace love's promise
and love's promises, now that our only
daughter's death has made shared sorrow the one
consolation that seems possible.
    I think she died because she could not hear
uplifting voices in the wind, because fresh snow
refused to speak to her, because the moon—

unlike the moonlight of our blurted vows—
was mute when it arose behind gray cliffs
the night she walked into the water and
was gone; for her stirred trees were merely trees;
warmed stones around a campfire merely stones,
not witnesses, not friends or guardians.
The story how we fell in love, inspired
by that mad moose, never could make her laugh
or make her seek a story of her own.

     And now that I think back again, I see
that moose rump disappear into the woods;
I see the twisted oak and maple leaves
close in behind him in the woven shade,
with nothing left for us to dwell upon
but your carved statue on the mantelpiece.

MONKEY EVOLUTION

First I'll describe what happened yesterday,
and then, my dear, I'll make my huge request.
After my guest appearance in her class
in which I argued most persuasively,
I must admit, that Darwin's bold idea,
Descent by Natural Selection, has
explanatory power no other theory
showing what we are can emulate,
Professor Dunn described her husband's job—
teaching Capuchin monkeys how to help
disabled people who can't use their hands,
bringing them water, answering the phone,
keeping them company. Across the hall
in the new lab, the monkey crouched upon
her husband's shoulder, bright-eyed, curious,
and then as I approached, she suddenly
leapt out toward me, entwined her skinny arms
around my neck and held me tight as if
she never would let go. Although surprised,
Professor Dunn's admiring husband said:
Like humans, monkeys also fall in love
irrationally at first sight, and I
was designated to be honored so.
Deep in my mind I heard the surging swell
of Richard Wagner's masterful duet
when Tristan and Isolde, those lost lovers
in the dwindling night, wholly embrace
their single destiny. I blush to think
that I was flattered, and I wonder now
what wayward monkey intuition brought
her sudden passion on. She snatched the pen
from my shirt pocket and then raced away
while looking back to see if I would try

to follow and retrieve the pen back, laughing—
I'm sure that's what her chirping meant—as if
she knew love ought to end in play. Right then
I wanted a Capuchin of my own
and so I called our Vet to ask what is
involved in caring for a monkey pet.

     He told me they are prone to catching cold,
that they are always bumping into things
and breaking bones. The greatest cause of death
in monkey ancestors, falling from trees,
he said, accounts for why the fear of falling
to this day still haunts our human dreams;
what's more, they never can be housebroken,
you have to diaper them throughout the day,
since, unlike wolves, monkeys evolved in trees,
so when they pooped the problem wasn't theirs,
they didn't have to learn to clean things up.

     Consider this: owning a monkey is
like having a rambunctious two-year old
living forever in your house. You think
that even for the tender sake of love
you can contend with that? And now, my dear,
for my delayed request: I must confess
that I can't manage such a pet alone;
now that our kids are grown and gone,
now that the bloom of youth has left a pallor
in our cheeks, I need you to agree
that we'll adopt a monkey for our home.

     A big advantage is you won't compete
for my attention or my loyalty,
not after all these operatic years.
Can you imagine that I'd love you less,
or that I'd ask for a divorce—a joke,
that's just a joke—should you reject me now?

BOBCAT

I'm glad you're glad that I've returned on time.
A whole week camping in the woods alone
restores my spirits and renews my hope
we'll find a way to save the wilderness.

It's been a year since Bill and Sue drove out
to spend their anniversary with us,
and Sue just sent this photograph to me;
I'm not sure that you know the wildlife story
that's behind it, but you must recall
the chef and owner of the Lakeside Lodge
purchased a baby bobcat years ago
and I would go there just to play with him.

He took to me, which worried you because
the game he most enjoyed when I'd sit still
inside his pen was sneaking up behind
my back to wrap his careful paws around
my neck and rub his cheek against my ear.
But in the wild, that's how all bobcats hunt
their prey where one bite ends a rabbit's life;
the hair-tufts on their ears help them to hear.

We slowly strolled beside the frozen lake
that spring before the lodge reopened
for the tourist trade, watching an osprey ride
the thermal tides. The restless cat must have
escaped its cage—an eager male will seize
on any opportunity to mate
throughout the year, though females come in heat
mainly in February or in March—
and stalking in the silence of the woods,
it must have heard me there, and out it came
full speed to where we stood. Sue screamed—
her voice still curdles in my memory—
and when the bobcat leaped into my arms,
she nearly passed out on that very spot.

I can't contain the mischief in my heart,
and what I fabricated to them then
was that all animals respond to me
this trusting way, instinctively assuming
that I am their friend. I let that fiction
hover in the frosty air for just
an instant more, then I confessed my fib—
that I had known the cat since it was only
three months old. I still was holding him,
and that's when Sue, revived although still pale,
took out her camera and snapped the picture
that I'm showing you right now. I'd like
to nurture every creature in the world—
we need protection, we need mothering—
though more affection between you and me
might help alleviate my fears about
the prospect for our species if we can't
learn to control our greed, our lust
to dominate, subdue, control. Do you
remember that the bobcat only lived
till summertime when it was struck down
on the highway by a driver in the night?

THE CRACKED APPLE TREE

Right on that branch we saw the snowy owl
the one time it arrived from Canada.
Don't cut it down! I know it's past the age
for bearing useful fruit; it crowds the house
and darkens both the upstairs rooms, but we
have changed the place enough—the well is new,
the paneled walls, and all those shelves you built
are crammed with books. The day we bought the house
old Phillip put it in your mind to clear
the trees that blocked the vista to the west:
"People like to fix things up themselves,"
was what he said, and yet we've left it there
for over twenty years, just as you've left
his broken harrow rusting in the field
as if it were a piece of sculpture, though
it's like the rib cage of a dinosaur.

Old Phillip was afraid to cut it down;
he told me that he saw a girl's ghost there
whose lover murdered her when she got pregnant.
She lived down the road before this house
replaced the one that burned, and Phillip said
that we can find a record of her death
tossed somewhere in the local files. Last week
when you were pruning it, you left your sweater
hanging on a branch, and when I took my walk
beside the stream before I went to bed,
I saw it flutter in the moonlit breeze
and thought of Phillip's story of the girl.

My father kept a bear's head in his den
over his desk: he teased me as a child,
pretending that the bear would talk to him.
I never found out if he shot the bear.

I know you like to watch that great stone ridge,
framed by the distant Adirondack range,
after the brittle leaves have fallen down.
I've seen you sit beside the window, staring
at the long striations—yellow, tan, and brown
turning to orange as the sun comes up—
as if you saw something you couldn't share.
I've warned the children not to bother you
when you take on that inward mood of yours.

What if a blizzard drives the snowy owl
down here again, and he can't find his branch?
What if the man returns, filled with remorse,
seeking his lover by our apple tree?
One can't be certain such things don't occur.
Your books are full of mysteries and puzzles,
half-invented memories, and choices
that can't be explained. You'll never know for sure
if Phillip made the murder story up
about the pregnant girl as an excuse
to leave the tree uncut. You'll never know
if I invented father's talking bear.
I saw the look that crossed your face when I
told you about the girl; I'm certain you
were ready then to let me have my way.

You leave the harrow lying in the field;
you keep your thoughts about the layered ridge
and what its colored lines remind you of,
and let me keep the cracking apple tree
for our love's sake. For if you don't, my dear,
I'll put my wedding nightgown on and stand
there in the moonlight on the tree-stump, still
as your ridge, as if I were a snowy owl.

NURSING AND DREAMING

Why must you nurse him in the living room?
Waking alone in bed confuses me;
I think I'm dreaming or I'm somewhere else.
You have been gone over an hour, dozing
in my old chair. The fire is almost out;
the groaning down-draft makes it smoky here.
I'll warm some milk for you, then come to bed!
He'll sleep unless the dead elm's cracking branches
startle him. Or did I dream that too,
with mother standing at the open door,
my brother in her arms, her smooth white legs
shining with their own light? I heard the rain
behind her and the creaking trees as if
someone—the wind?—were following her there.
        Again tonight I woke and couldn't tell
the baby's wailing from the wind. I switched
the lion's-head lamp on by the bed; it yawned,
and then I saw my father's silence in
its opal eyes. Drink up your milk before
it's cold! I want to finish the same dream
that started when our son was born—about
my brother coming home—the night I saw
you staring through the down-pour at the elm
as if you'd nursed here in another life;
I promised you I'd take it down to stop
the wind from blowing branches on the house.
        Can't you nurse him in bed so I don't have
to ramble through the house in search of you?
I used to sleep-walk when I was a child.
His cries wake me up anyway, or else
I hear the door-latch click no matter how
you try to close it quietly. There's something
you don't want to say, and yet I sense
I'm dreaming what you wish for me to dream.

Your body's changed, your breasts, but I can't tell
my unchanged body how to wait for your
return. I'm no one in my dream or I'm
not me. My father's death lurks in the elm,
although that figure past the door reminds
me of my father too—unless he is
the both of us combined. You don't appear
as my own wife, I feel I've lost you and
myself, though here you are, nursing our child,
with real wind clacking branches in the elm
and drizzle misting in the garden rocks.
        Finish your milk—then let's go back to bed;
tomorrow, if the wind is still, I'll cut
the dead elm down and bury the dry stump.

SECRETS

I doubt that you remember her—except
that final summer when we took the house
beside the bay. I vowed to wait until
right now to tell you how your mother died.
Do you still have her photograph—the one
in which her hands are cupped, with you trying
to peek inside? Every morning even
before I woke, she took you for a walk
to search for starfish scattered on the beach.
You were excited after you returned,
but then you'd sink into a sudden gloom
without a cause that I could see; you'd go
into your room and sit there with your shells,
arranging them in boxes; you'd stay inside
all afternoon. At night your mother talked
about your moods, though in your room, I thought,
when playing with your shells, you seemed content.
      You had one smooth quartz stone, your favorite,
and every time we looked you had it placed
inside another box. A thousand times
your mother asked me what I thought that meant.
I thought the stone meant you; the boxes meant
your made-up lives. Your mother thought the stone
was her—that you were putting her away—
but never told you what she guessed. Claiming
they were all beautiful, especially
the rounded stone, you scared us when you said
it was the only one that had itself
inside itself. The way your mouth was fixed
warned us to inquire no more. Your mother
wept all night; we held each other, kissing
gently in the dark, though something private
deep in her sobbing tightened her. She said:
"I don't know why I haven't done things right."

I promised her we'd take a trip, and when
her spirits rose, it seemed to me that you
no longer switched the stone from box to box.
     We flew down to Bermuda where we took
a cabin by the beach. At night we strolled
the curving shore, collecting colored stones
and sea-shells to bring home, or curled together,
hugging, naming whatever stars we knew.
She told me things I'd never heard—like once
her mother ran off with her father's friend.
One moonlit evening we undressed each other
on the beach to take a swim. We raced
into the water, holding hands, and then
I let her go so I could watch. Flawless
as polished marble, oh her smooth arms gleamed,
plunging like dolphins as she dove; wind gusts
blew clouds across the moon, and she was gone.
     "Didn't you search for her?" the captain asked,
"Couldn't she swim?" "The water was so dark,"
I said, "and yes, she grew up by the sea."
"Was she depressed?" he asked, and I assured him
she was never happier. "Strange tides,"
I thought I heard him say. Sometimes I dream
that she gets washed up further down the beach,
having forgotten who she is and who
we are, and that she is alive, living
another life. And then I am awake,
wishing something familiar—like the feel
of stone—might bring us back to her. We must
forget the past; we have a new life now.
Alice loves you—she's all you really know
since she moved in with us. Can you recall
your clinging to her on our wedding day,
helping her unpack? You kept the picture
of her sitting on her mother's lap.

I didn't tell you how your mother died
because so much remained unknown. Promise
never to tell Alice—she's heard enough.
This has to be our secret; promise me.
This little golden starfish—take it, Joan—
I've saved it for the necklace that I gave you
when you turned thirteen; your mother bought it
by herself the day before she died.
She said that having secrets was her way
of holding on, and that you'd understand.

FERNS BY THE WATERFALL

    I knew you'd marry again. Mom's been dead
two years, and I'm prepared. She'd sit there on
that ledge beside the pool; she loved to read
while savoring an orange or a pear
as I was catching tadpoles like a boy,
searching for salamanders under logs.
I always had to call her twice before
she'd hear and lift her head up from her book—
as if she wasn't quite sure where we were.
Janet has hiked back here with me; she's seen
the pool swirling below the waterfall.
She took her clothes off once and dove right in.

    Don't feel obliged to ask if it's all right
with me for you to marry—you're still young,
you have your needs; no one should live alone
or die alone. If you love Janet, marry her,
she can decide whether your doctoring
will leave you time for her. What troubles me
is how Mom died. Why did she go alone
to swim at night so late in September
under the waterfall? She never went
there by herself before. When she got home,
shivering to the bone, she woke me up
to ask if I would rub her back and arms;
I couldn't break out of my dream in which
somebody—maybe you—was strangling her,
and I still have the strangest feeling that
the dream repeated something I once saw.
I'll wake at night, thinking I hear her moan,
and then I see you in the hospital,
your stethoscope around your neck like some
great spider hanging from its threads, saying:
"We doubt there is a link between the chill
and what shock later caused her heart to stop."

Soon I'll be leaving home, I'm seventeen;
there's more I need to know. Why did I dream
of someone strangling mother on the night
she stole off to my waterfall? Climbing
a ridge, trying to escape from someone,
she called out, but no words would come, only
slobbering sounds. And as I woke, wanting
to help her with the words, just as he reached
her throat and covered her, I dove into
the pool, and heard those sounds on my own lips.
I still feel that I stutter when we talk.
    Had I seen Janet before mother died?
She's not like Mom at all; she'd rather hike
than read or listen to a symphony;
she knows the names of ferns: elk's horn, hare's foot,
and maidenhair. I can't imagine how
you met, and yet it seems I know her from
another life. I saw her watching me
when we were naked in the pool. "Look how
the light reflecting from the water makes
the birch limbs dance"; then coming close she gazed
at me, a long, slow gaze: "Bird's nest," she said
as if her list was now complete. Mother
also loved ferns, but not out in the wild;
her flowers were arranged, circled by ferns,
yellow balancing blue, and with a touch
of purple or red. Nature, for her taste,
didn't make the right designs, squandering
its precious colors unwatched in the woods.
    I've needed us to sit beside the pool,
listening to the waterfall, before
you marry Janet; and I'll pick some ferns
for us to eat tonight. Before she had
the killing stroke, we were alone, and Mom
asked in the hospital: "The ferns, I need
to know all of their names." April's the time

when they begin uncurling into fronds;
now that they're tender, they're called fiddleheads.
The names—we've got to learn to get them right!

INHERITANCE

   I'm worried that you want to go in debt
to me, buying yourself a partnership
in Arthur's firm. It's only two years since
you've earned your architect's degree. I know
he is your friend, but friendship's not engraved
in blood, and your assurance that you'll pay
me back . . . well, sons can't pay their fathers back
unless they give the same love to their sons,
and on until some final reckoning.
But what I care about is now—you're home;
it's been three winters since we've split some wood
together as we used to do, and there
are red pines I've transplanted from the field
I want to show to you. Only yesterday
a ruffed grouse crashed against the window and
mother decided it would make the right
Thanksgiving meal for your return. "It's like
the sacrificial ram, caught in the brush,
God gave to Abraham for Sarah's sake,"
was what she said. I let that pass; you know
what weight your mother likes to lay on things.
   The last year you were home she got so damn
possessive that I found myself competing
for your love. And then I felt left out.
She has a stronger hold on you than I.
Some day you'll feel your own life flowing in
your son, and then your debt will be redeemed.
One cool October afternoon, when he
is splitting dried-out wood with you, and you
are resting on a stump beside the sumac
blazing in the last warmth of the sun,
he'll take his T-shirt off, and as the axe
descends, you'll watch his shoulder muscles flex

and then release beneath his flawless skin.
A waterfall, you'll flow out of yourself,
and what you are will find its form returned—
as if the wind blew leaves back to the trees.

    Don't be embarrassed that I tell you this;
it hurts for me to fumble with the words,
but it hurts happily, and that's the best
I have to give. Since you've been gone, I've planted
blight-resistant raspberries, too much
for us to use, but mother says she'll send
you her preserves. It has been hard, without
your help, to get the apples sprayed. We hope
you'll find a place where you can work nearby.
Arthur would not approve of that. I doubt
he understands what homes are for; he left
his father's farm to start his own. That's why
your mother takes the grouse to be a sign
to cherish your return, and why she made me
spray the raspberries all summer long.

    We've got another hour before it's dark;
let's split more wood. The farmer's almanac
predicts sub-zero cold again this year.
The planet's changed. My father warned me: "Son,
the reckoning will come. Earth is our home
or else our grave." Those were his words. It was
a day like this, and we were raking leaves
still dazzling in their reds and golds. I stood
before him, naked to the waist, sweating,
thinking of your mother, trying to decide
what I would say when I proposed to her.

REMAINS

My ship departs next Saturday, Ruth knows
I have to go. This time, Dad, keep in touch.
We'll study whales, both stranded and alive;
their great intelligence, how they maintain
communication over distances
with sonic pictures showing what they feel
from sounds produced—they have no vocal cords—
within their lungs. Think of it, Dad, pictures
of what they feel from sequences of clicks!
Their brains are larger than a man's; the links
connecting stimuli to response are
inexhaustible; their memories possess
a power we can barely comprehend.
Professor Singer says they demonstrate
a vast capacity to show affection.
　　Tell Mom that Ruth and I have broken up;
I'll write to her. Mom warned me once that Ruth
could not accept my love because Ruth feels
she isn't worthy to be loved. And now
I'm not sure what remains to be explained.
Ruth kept accusing me—though it's not true—
of loving someone else, and yet perhaps
I did hold something back. She'd say: "All you
talk about is whales." But we're killing them!
A hundred tons of pain with each harpoon!
Millions of years evolved what Cousteau calls
"extraordinary gentleness." No whale
will hurt a diver if he's not attacked,
and yet we're killing them! The great blue whale's
almost extinct. I can't accept a future
with no whales remaining in the sea,
but Ruth won't get involved, although she knows
what sorrow is. And if I write to Mom

to say I've got to help the whales, she'll think
that's my excuse for leaving Ruth. Not so.
Our species can't embrace our mortal lives,
and killing makes us feel omnipotent.

   The twenty-pound harpoon grenade explodes
inside their flesh. Reports describe their cry—
part howl, part plea; they dive down, opening
the hooks which gouge their organs out. They're dragged
back bobbing to the ship. The sea swirls red;
the air takes on a fiery haze. You know
the whale is dead when its gigantic mouth
opens as if it were about to speak.
A whale will swim between an injured whale
and the harpooning ship; or if he's hurt
and has become a burden to the herd,
he may decide to stop his breath and die.
It's difficult for whales to mate because
they're too huge to plunge in like simians;
there's pain in their repeated, strained attempts.
Whales breath like us, so they must rise and sink
together as they try to merge, using
their flippers to embrace each other's bulk.
Often the sea clouds with defeated sperm.
Gray whales require a second male to help,
to lie across the coupling pair so they
can keep their balance in the churning sea.
Ruth wonders how they've managed to survive
through the millennia. Mom thinks such mating
shows they are incapable of love.

   You've got to hear the whales sing, hundreds
with modulating voices: mewings, trills,
janglings and whoops, creakings and bellowings,
each making its own sounds for the sheer joy
of making sounds. Lagorio remarked
"It's a cathedral in the sea!" We can't

explain those alternating calls, unless
they're joining with the family of whales.
     When I left Ruth, I pictured you and Mom,
still young, in your first house, and lost myself
thinking that I was you, imagining
you could foresee you'd have me as your son.
The swaying bed became a whale, holding
me there, more buoyant than I'd ever felt,
and all the whales were singing, praising me.

TRILLIUM

Maybe I shouldn't tell you this—you are
his daughter, Beth, as much as you are mine—
I think your father's having an affair.
Last spring he started hiking in the woods,
just as he used to do when you were born;
he said he needed time to be alone.
But then I noticed he began to mention
subtle things about the flowers—details.
"Everything about the trillium comes
in threes," he said, "petals, sepals, stigmas;
the ovate leaves, all three of them, whorl right
below the triple shining crimson flowers."
    He'd follow me around the house, describing
what he'd seen, and get annoyed with me
if I did not respond enough. Last week
I couldn't help myself; I blurted out:
"What do you want to say to me?" I see
you're skeptical, and yet you know your father
well enough to sense when he is holding
something back. Why should the fact a flower
has suggestive names—like wake-robin,
stinking benjamin, wet-dog trillium—
be so significant to him, unless
there's a confession in those names, hiding
even from himself? He says wake-robin
is its name because it blossoms just as
spring arrives. I think he feels that spring
can come again for him. At our age, Beth,
men often have the need to start again,
and you'd be wrong to think your father's not
like other men. You love the wilderness
and gardening; you know the wild flowers' names
and when to plant the lettuce and the peas.
Why can't he take you sometimes on his walks?

I figured you'd get angry if I spoke
what's really on my mind. Lately you have
so little patience when I try to share
my thoughts with you—as if our being close
threatens your sense of who you are. I'm sure
you know that stinking benjamin describes
the odor of the trillium—it's like
a sweating body, a body dying
or making love is what he didn't say.
I'm asking only for your empathy,
not condemnation of his so-called walks.
No daughter ever loved herself unless
she loved her mother also. Beth, I'm scared,
I don't know how to meet this need of his,
and I'm too old to start again—not old,
but old enough to want to keep the loves
I've built upon: his love, my dear, and yours.
And his remaining here gives both of us
the needed distance it's so good to cross.

　　　Remember how the two of us would bake
his birthday cake? I'd let you split the eggs,
and you'd sit on the kitchen counter, spreading
thick brown fudge in swirls, touching my lips
with one delicious finger. You believe
all this is fantasy—that father's walks
are innocent? What has he said to you?
I think you're keeping something to yourself.

　　　When you were in my womb, you'd press your head
against the pulsing of my artery.
You were the hardest child to get to bed,
and when from sheer exhaustion you let go,
your lips would tighten and expose your teeth,
your mouth turn downward with a little drool;
I'd stand there looking, baffled by such sleep.

　　　Is there a chance he'll leave me for this girl?
What do you think? We haven't talked like this

in years—about the birds and flowers, no less!
We make a funny triangle: husband,
wife, and trillium—till trillium do
us part. Thanks for the smile—I need it now,
and promise not to ask what else you know
about my rival, wet-dog trillium.

PIANO

When Dick left on his trip last week, and I
moved in with you and Dad so you could help
while I was nursing Sue, I heard you play
for the first time, and learned Dad bought it as
a wedding gift. Why have you waited all
these years to play again? I don't mean to
invade your privacy, but a daughter
has a friend's right to show she cares. I've watched
your ritual of setting hyacinths
upon the piano-top before you play;
you breathe so deeply that it seems the notes
come back to you right from the flowers' scent.
Has my return affected you this way?
        But now I have a daughter of my own;
I also know what things a wife can't tell
her husband, not exactly things she's done,
but things she's thought. Though Dad loves music, still
he seems uneasy when you play; he pulls
his ear and puts a finger in his mouth.
I want to share with you, while Dick's away,
my mother-fear of being smothered by
the people I love most. How much do you
reveal to Dad? Have you suggested that
there may be ties between my coming home
and your piano playing after almost
thirty years? At Dick's goodbye, he stood there
in the windy, sunlit doorway; yellow
and red maple leaves swirled into the house
as if his parting were their chance to make
themselves at home. And then he handed me
the hyacinths. That night when I moved back
to spend this month with you, Dad said, "Their smell
gets stronger after they begin to droop."

I didn't notice then that no one played;
the piano stood in its own space as if
the silence needed shape to hold the thoughts
we couldn't share. Before Dick left, he wanted
to describe his business friend in Rome:
"We're so alike, it's weird, but Phil's wife is
your opposite. Last visit, after she
had gone to bed, I read her diary;
'Dick is a warm, informal man,' she wrote,
'but somehow I don't trust him in my house.'"
Dick might have told that story either as
denial or confession; or it may
have been his hinting that he trusted me.

I ought to understand why you're released
to play the piano now. Something I need
to know about myself is hidden there;
music must be your way of telling me.
I still suspect that Dad dislikes the scent
of hyacinths, although he used to read
me ancient tales before I went to sleep—
of Hyacinthus' blood that was transformed
into a purple flower by Apollo
who had killed his friend by accident.

But when Dad listens to you play, a frown
like yours creasing his face, and his fingers
keeping time or twitching on his stiff knee,
maybe he thinks of losses you and he
have shared—maybe my leaving home. Perhaps
it's not for me you're playing, but for him?

Look, there it is—I'm sure that is the oak
we built our tree-house in the final summer
Grandpa was alive. The tree-house that
you built might be more accurate; you never
let me hammer; passing nails was my job.
    Thanks for not asking why I brought you here;
maybe as my brother you can sense
what's troubling me. Those summers on the farm—
we were close then, with Grandma watching us:
"You've got to take your sister," she would say,
"a family is like a hand—fingers
are useless one by one." Sit here with me
beneath the oak, I want to try to talk.
    I haven't been myself—I'm pregnant and
I don't know if the father's John or Bill.
I thought I'd better wait to choose which one
to marry till I slept with both, and now,
whichever one I choose, it would be like
marrying two men; the other's ghost
would be there in my bed—and in my child.
    I'm thinking of not keeping it—it's still
only a little hungry speck of cells.
Should I discuss this with both John and Bill?
And what if one says "Yes," the other "No"?
Last week, when I had lunch with Dad, I felt
I'd lost hold of myself. He was about
to pay the bill when suddenly he looked
much younger than he's looked in years—his face
seemed smooth, his nose more aquiline, like yours,
his lips more curved and tilted to the left.
And then I thought: "My God, what if he's not
my father after all?" Now do you see?—
I've lost my sense of what it's safe to trust.

It's crazy, but the hardest thing for me
to talk about is that I feel it's you
who are to blame for this. Remember how
you made me bait your hooks when we hiked down
to fish in Grandpa's pond for perch and bass?
They'd wriggle to get free; how could they know
that it was not my fault? I still can't stand
the taste of fish, the crumbly meat. Sometimes
I'd sneak off to the tree-house by myself
and make believe you'd gone off on a trip;
I wrote the letters that you sent to me.
Then Grandpa left and died away from home,
and Grandma wouldn't talk of him. She'd weave
until the window light would fade, and say:
"This is the best work that I've ever done."

How did you get her tapestry from Dad?
Dad always claimed that it belonged to him.
But Grandma liked to weave things in for us:
I'm sure that tall oak in the woods behind
the farmhouse is our tree, and those white specks,
like trickling light among the rounded leaves,
maybe they're you and me. You should have told me
Grandpa left to die; he was afraid
we'd see him broken at the end. And yet
what I suspected was much worse. Always
something is missing that I need to know.

After the farm was sold, you didn't seem
to care for me as much, or notice me,
and it's been years since I've asked for your help.
After my lunch with Dad, that whirling night,
still feeling that I couldn't trust myself
and therefore couldn't keep the child, I dreamed
I pulled a baby out of Grandpa's pond;
it had your face. It stood up, waved goodbye,
and walked away into the yellow house
of Grandma's tapestry. Maybe the reason

I can't decide is that I never knew
whether you had to love me—was it me?—
or was it love for Grandma's sake. That's what
I mean, there's always something I don't know!
        What difference can it make to you to know
who my child's father is? I'm sure, if you
adopted it, Grandma's ghost would say:
"I'll weave it into my next tapestry;
a family must hold together like
a hand." Then I could try to start again.
Just ask your wife, I know she'll understand;
some women can't have children of their own.

CLEANING THE FISH

Mom says she won't; we'll have to clean them, though
she used to do it when I fished with Dad.
Dad's illness wore her down; I think she felt
relief after he died, and didn't mourn
him long enough before she married Sam.
    I know there is an art to cleaning fish.
In ancient times, prophets could look into
the future by examining the entrails
of an animal; they'd burn it then
to satisfy their chosen deity.
    Hold down the tail, and use a scraping knife,
stroking the scales to get right to the skin.
Slice through the vent and open up the fish,
just like a box. Then pluck the organs out:
liver, bladder, stomach and gills; cut off
the head and tail, and wash away the blood.
This tissue here—this iridescent film
that runs along the whole backbone—must be
removed with care. How smooth the small heart is!
It will continue beating for a while.
    Fish don't feel pain like people do; they go
right into shock without the fear of death,
like other animals, because they have
no thought of time extending after them.
They don't know what loss is; you mustn't feel
sorry for them. Don't be upset with Mom.
It was because of us that she remarried
so soon following Dad's death. She knew
we needed money and a healthy father
in the house after those draining years.
    When Sam bought you that dress with yellow birds
you've wanted for a year, you hardly said
a word of thanks. But I predict that he'll

be kind to you and Mom. I've told him how
Dad sang to you before you went to bed,
even when he had lost the melody,
until the very end. Sam understands
the way the dead still live within our minds.

   The clearest memory I have of Dad—
he's pasting in his stamps, studying them
with his magnifying glass, looking for
the special marks that make them valuable.
The ones he loved the most were animals,
bright red and blue, I think from Africa.
He told me that he never traded those.
I saved his whole collection for a while,
but then I had to sell it to a friend.

   Enough of that! Today we concentrate
on fish! First, rinse it in cold water, dry,
then lightly rub with salt, inside and out.
A shallow dish is what we use, and top
with sherry, soy, and peanut oil. Later,
I'll give you the measurements. Sprinkle
with parsley, garnish with some shredded scallions,
and, behold, a two pound fish should steam
for twenty minutes and be done! Take out
Mom's crystal glasses, Grandma's silverware,
the yellow tablecloth, and light the candles
when the sun goes down; they shine with orange
merging into purple blue, almost like
the inside of the fish. When you grow up
and marry someone whom you really love,
you'll teach your daughter how to clean a fish.

   If Dad were still with us, he'd show approval
with his eyes: "Life must serve life," they'd say,
"here's to good food!" And Sam, well we'll find out
whether he has an appetite for fish!

BROTHER TO BROTHER

I bought these garden shears for you to help
me to explain the time I took Dad's shears
and told him I last saw them in your room.
I meant to borrow them to cut barbed wire—
I knew they weren't made for that—but when
I chipped the blade, I panicked and then threw
them in the pond. Dad's anger flustered you;
you stood there with your hand over your mouth,
though maybe you were laughing—I don't know.
        For years I've asked myself if this were worth
confessing; yet last night I dreamed your son
had found the shears while diving in the pond
for turtles, and again I felt the need
to ask for your forgiveness—just as when
I told your wife you used to make me sneak
into their room at night to see if they
were making love. Everyone fears the dark;
what's wrong is that I dwell on it too much.
Some common sight—like sprouting corn planted
in rows across the field to the wood's edge,
each shadow a hieroglyph upon the earth—
can make me cry out with a surging wish
to hold that scene forever in my mind.
You're so absorbed designing houses that
you don't have time to think how long we're dead.
        Maybe Dad's death disturbs me more than you
because I see myself in him, and when
he punished you, although I took his shears,
I guessed that you resented both of us.
He loved repairing things around the house,
but first he loved to prune his apple trees.
He'd eye a branch, his arm outstretched, holding
his breath until he knew exactly how

he wanted it, then snip as if its life
depended on it. "Light, it needs more light!"
he'd say to me, and snip again. And yet
to picture him alive reminds me that
he's dead—I just can't get my grief to end.

      Sometimes I envy you. You seem to watch
yourself as if you were somebody else,
amused with what you see. But I still see
Dad's pruning shears, poised for another snip,
catching the light; the circle of moist wood
at the cut apple branch, catching the light.

You've shared too much to leave Jim now. Is it
another man? I've paid the price for searching
for a perfect love, as mother warned.
Remember how she loved to put things by?
Each jar was packed with still another bean
or cucumber; she'd say: "There's always room
for just one more." There always was. I still
can picture her preserves: blueberry jam,
strawberry jam, raspberry, cherry, quince,
tomato sauces, jar after steaming jar,
the tiny seeds sparkling like yellow stars
in their red galaxy. She placed the jars
in open shelves where everyone could see,
row after row, in greens, in blues, in shades
of red and orange. "That's my rainbow,"
she would say, "I'm Mrs. Noah, maybe
you've heard of me." Living alone, what can
you prove by that? We all need someone's help.
       Can you repair your plumbing, wire your stove?
Accepting help from strangers can't protect
you from the need for love. I've learned to live
with emptiness, watching the sea, and that's
my strength, though I can fill the morning hours
when I write with characters invented
for my book. I make them suffer as I
weep for them. Like you, one leaves her husband;
she regrets it only later when her
daughter does the same. After her father's
sudden death, she visits her old mother
to tell her that she's met a novelist,
fallen in love, and wants to live with him.
Her mother is preserving fruit. She warns
her daughter: married love is what a lifetime

must embrace, especially shared sorrow.
Holding an empty jar, framed by the window
where evening sun streams through in dusty beams,
she says she loved her husband to the end
when all those plums and peaches, luminous
in their juices, and labeled in her print
to give their dates, lined her kitchen shelves.

Don't leave Jim for another man; please read
my book; I think some parts are funny—like
when mother, Mrs. Noah in the book,
decides to breed angora rabbits, but
each one of them turns out to be a girl.
The pet store owner I make up remarks
there's little difference for the naked eye
to see, and Mrs. Noah falls in love
and sleeps with him, just once, right in the store
with all the puppies yelping in their pens.
The last scene, which I still may change, will show
the daughter's daughter, packing blueberries,
asking if happy endings can be true.

But you're my sister! You know if you have
to leave him, if you really must; for just
a little while, you could move in with me.

COINCIDENCE

Don't be alarmed! Let me sit here with you
to watch the waterfall. It may sound like
I'm telling you a tale, but listen, please,
then maybe you'll believe that I'm sincere,
and this coincidence, finding you here
beside this rocky pool, leaning against
this ancient tree with evening light reflecting
off the water on your face as if
you were the image of the waterfall,
may have some special meaning for us both.

I met a girl, a year ago, sitting
where you sit now, her chin upon one knee,
like a statue, arms wrapped around her legs.
I told her she reminded me of someone
I once loved who died within her sleep.
She let me talk and liked my company,
and seemed to understand my grief as if
it were her own. I could have sworn her eyes
were moist when speckled light reflected on them
from the waterfall. She lived at home
out by the bay, but worked not far from me,
and she agreed to meet for lunch next week
by the stone lion at the library.

I waited angry for an hour, fearing
someone had pushed her on the subway tracks.
Maybe she got the date wrong; maybe she too
had waited, felt abandoned, and gone home?
How could I know? And then I realized
I wasn't certain that I knew her name.
Laurel, had she said Laurel? I wasn't sure.
Could Laurel be her last name? What had I
to go on otherwise? And so I called
the Laurels listed in the Bayside phone book—

five every night. The tenth try that I made
brought me her voice in a subdued "Hello"
that seemed to echo from some distant cave.
One second I was sure, but then she said:
"There's no Miss Laurel here." I realized,
abashed, I knew the voice—I must have called
my mother's house. Pretending innocence,
I said "Excuse me please," and left the phone,
wondering if she knew that it was me.

　　　　Having run out of Laurels, I then tried
some other names of other plants or flowers,
randomly selected, for I figured
coincidence was now my only hope.
And yet I always asked "Is Laurel home?"
One night a voice replied "Miss Laurel died
over a year ago." I hung up trembling,
never made another call. But then
I dreamed Laurel sat by the pond where first
I saw her just as you sit now. Slowly,
as if I floated step by nearing step
along the mossy path, I reached to touch her
when she turned to me and raised her arms.
Her eyes and mouth were blurred—as if reflected
upon water, moving as the water moved,
murmuring, but not with words. A lion
resting on a rock, guarding his high cave,
nodded: if I returned I'd find you here.

　　　　I knew I'd see the pond-light on your face;
I knew the waterfall along the stones
would echo human sounds—calling sounds
and pleasure sounds. I'm sure I've seen that lion's
look of sorrow on your face before.
Can you believe me though you may suspect
I've read this story somewhere in a book?
While this light lasts, maybe you'll let me touch
your lips, and then you'll tell me who *you* are.

THE HOMECOMING

You need to know I knew that John was ill;
I never meant to keep this to myself.
Although we hoped to reach Maine before dark,
the farm my father sold some twenty years ago
was only fifteen miles off our route,
and John turned off the highway as I asked.
It's time, I thought, to tell him why we had
to leave the farm. He sulked a little as
I stroked his finger with the silver scar
just like a ring; he felt we had delayed
this holiday too long. When we arrived,
a cold gust swung the cedar gate; John laughed:
"Your mother's ghost is welcoming you back."

    The house was only used in summer time;
it was locked now, although a lantern burned
over the entry door and from the upstairs
where my bedroom was, to warn off hunters
now that hunting season had begun.
I looked inside; a hat hung on a chair
resembling the plaid cap my father wore.
Behind the house a row of apple trees
had gone unpruned and wild for all these years;
our tree-house in the oak had lost one side.

    A tense red squirrel watched us as we crunched
along the path to find the spring-fed pond
we stocked with bass. Though shrunken now, more slime
along the edge, its border willow-stand
composed a golden web against the sky.
On Casting Rock my brother got a fishhook
wedged in his palm; I still can see his hand—
the swelled, blue spots where both barbs entered in.

    Talking to you now, trying to decide
if we're right for each other, I recall

John bent behind the boulder, scraping mud
from his grooved boots, but watching me. Even
without turning my head, I sensed he watched.
I stared at dry leaves thrashing in the pond,
then closed my eyes. "We owned a mare," I said,
"who nuzzled her foal and licked its nose and ears,"
and John, as if he read my mind, exclaimed:
"We have our own child now. It's time to go!"
He pulled my glove off, gripped my whitened hand,
and tried to lead me briskly past the house;
the door-lock must have sprung as it used to
when sudden wind blasts speared down from the north.
"Let's look around, just quickly," I implored.

      The red hat on the chair was not my father's,
yet I could picture his flushed ears, flaming
as if his blood had angered in his veins
when he returned from hunting in the dusk.
We went into the kitchen where we found
opened soup cans—just as rifle shots cracked
across the hill. We wondered if strangers
had broken in or had the legal owners
hunted there? I felt John must be told,
and I commanded "Follow me!" in tones
I'd never heard in my own throat before.

      Steep as I remembered, we climbed the stairs
to where my parents slept. "It happened there,"
my low voice murmured. "They were arguing.
Their shouting woke us. We crouched beside the door
clutching each other. Mother glared at him,
then cupped her hand over the candle flame
as if to catch the light, as if to hold
and keep some needed warmth. And father stared.
I heard flesh sizzle. I can smell it still,
and I can hear her scream circling the room
around my head. Then somehow I was somewhere
far away; and now I'm here with you,

trying to tell you so I can forget."
"You should have told me long ago," John said;
"I'm not sure now I can believe it's true."

The hunters had returned with a huge buck
strapped to their jeep; its long tongue slipped across
its jaw, and its cut belly steamed as if
 the dead heart's final heat might warm the air.
John told them why we came, and led me back
as snowflakes wavered in the slate-blue dusk.
John died before he could be sure; I woke
beside him but he was already cold.

My son needs me; perhaps that's warmth enough
for any woman. I won't blame you if
you think it's wise for us to wait a while.

PATIENT TO DOCTOR

That young man in the other bed, I learned
his brain was damaged in an accident;
I heard his whimpering throughout the night
in garbled words that made no sense at all,
though his distress was clear enough.
There's not much you can do to fix my heart,
and since it's rumored that this hospital
has done the first successful brain transplant
and that you're looking for a volunteer,
I am your man. My mind is just as sharp,
just as inventive as it's ever been,
so you could substitute my mind for his,
accomplishing a double cure. The brain's
no different than other organs are,
just more complex, more functions to control—
tiny electric currents that can jump
across synaptic clefts. Of course I know
it needs a body to manipulate
to give the mind its own identity,
so, doctor, who then would I be, would I
be him and able to resume his life?
He'd have my memories, they'd still be mine,
and I'd still treasure them, but would they fit
the body they were in, and would his wife
accept him back as him? I'm sure that I could
learn to love his children, but would I
consider them as mine? Adapting—that's
what evolution taught us to do best;
I'll take this operation in my stride—
one more vicissitude intelligence
is challenged to accommodate. And if
his body's heart (which now is mine) gives out,
and it too suffers from decay, we could,

why not, in keeping, doctor, with your skill,
arrange another transplant to preserve
both me and my augmented memories
of children and my melancholy wife,
her shadow walking with her by the lake
as once upon a time we used to do?

DOCTOR TO PATIENT

I know your type; if you don't change your ways
you'll be back here much sooner than you think.
You are competing even when you try
to get yourself released in record time,
and you're competing when you joke
your heart's more metaphor than organ and
you're glad I am your surgeon since I was
an English major as a college youth.

Ah yes, I can recall reciting Keats
as I strolled through the quad in the crisp air,
and how exhilarating sorrow seemed
when so expressed. Our tastes are similar,
so maybe my compulsions are like yours
in that we seek perfection in our work.

But what I do saves lives, it's not just words,
though that must sound competitive to you.
While your heart hung there from a hook,
a gooey organ, nothing more, while I
was stitching in new arteries for you
before I placed it back into your chest,
I didn't think that I was "half in love
with easeful death;" to tell the truth,
I didn't give a damn for who you are
or who you love or what you'd miss if you
had chanced to die there under those cold lights.

Nothing about your heart is singular,
nothing about your longing is unique,
and humor is a universal balm.
My hard-learned skill was so impersonal
that I could readily have been replaced
by someone with the self-same skills,
and, strangely, that for me was ecstasy:
the sense I was both me and anyone—

I even could have been the patient, you,
just lying there with Keats's murmured words
inside my head. So can you match that thought
for taking pride in one's humility?

How's that for literary irony?
How's that for laughter of the gods? Maybe
there's really something curative in that—
your sense of curative, that the right words
add vigor to the beating of the heart
and make it stronger in its wish to live.

I can't believe you've drawn me into such
an argument with just a joke about
the heart as metaphor inspiring me
to quote lines that I once had memorized
long unrecoverable years ago,
as if performing surgery on you
were like revisiting a poem by Keats,
or like another life I might have lived.

AT THE TERMINAL

I have to change planes here, but I'm afraid
to fly again. We hit a down-draft over
the Rockies, plunging us a thousand feet
before we leveled out. Everyone screamed—
as if we had one voice that followed us
to testify what happened at the end.
All I could think was that we must be falling
faster than the speed of sound—nothing
about myself was in my mind. Death seemed
impersonal; I didn't feel embarrassed
when I wet my dress. The reason I
sat here by you with all these empty seats,
is I mistook you for Mom's doctor who
delivered me and cared for us since I
 was born. The likeness is remarkable,
although you're younger by at least ten years:
you have his sapphire eyes, his bony hands.

My ears throb like a fish washed on the beach;
I'll cover them when the next plane takes off—
or else I'll hear that scream. See what I mean?
Only a smoky wind was in my mind,
as if I'd never lived my life, as if
my father never said "We'll miss you" when
we kissed goodbye. There should have been pictures
with golden frames so I could think the times
I watched the sunrise with my brother from
our tree-house by the lake, hearing plink sounds
of leaping perch—plucked strings of a guitar;
or past my bed-hour, with Mom scolding him,
Dad led me to the "hooting grove" where owls
called out across the restless dark, responding
to their echoes or their mates. We'd try
to pick the call that started the replies,

but never could be sure. There always seemed
to be a first before the first we heard.
     "That's 'concourse wild of jocund din' for you!"
Dad would exclaim. I still can hear his voice
exactly, for I knew his words were not
meant to be understood. I should have thought
of them beneath the scream—Dad's moonlit teeth,
and wooing owl calls pleading in the night
their soothing, melancholy sound. My mind
was empty as the plane plunged down, and now
I feel I'm listening to someone else—
maybe it's mother's voice—talking to you,
although your stare tells me I'm beautiful.

     Mom said that all men fall in love with women
they have rescued, since men suffer from
some barrenness themselves they need to cure.
I think you're thinking that you'd like to spend
the night with me, and that I'd whisper little
owl songs in your ear, reminding you
of someone you once loved. These hollow noises
dizzy me—these voices gathering
with each departing plane. Why do they call
such places terminals? Nothing ends here!

     We're only passing through. I see your wife
waiting for you at home: she's peeling apples
in the sink as gold flecks on their skins recall
your eyes. She turns the faucet on and hears
the distant voice of someone she might marry
if your plane should crash, blushes, and then
returns to who she is, the naked apple
shining in her hand, not knowing that
beneath the long, pursuing scream, your last
framed picture was me talking to you here.

AT THE ECOLOGY
CONVENTION

Don't you remember me? It must have been
almost ten years ago—salmon fishing,
the Ryans' cabin up in Maine—that we
slept together. What are you doing here?
I'd heard you and your husband moved out west.
Your hair was darker then, you wore it straight,
and when you swam it covered up your face—
except your nose. You would pretend you had
to find your way back to the shore by smell.

Those red curls fooled me when I saw you here,
your grayish eyes seemed rounder, but noses
reveal one's inner self more than eyes do;
babies' noses all look the same. Have I
embarrassed you? That August night we met
the windy rain swirled right across the lake,
tore the boat loose, then suddenly it fell
so softly we could hear each hollow note
like bird calls underneath the eaves, and sniff
the odor wafting from the cedar woods.
You lay so still, your face framed in your arms,
repeating rain sounds with each breath, and then
you cried out in a moan: "Have you come back?"
I couldn't tell if you called in your dream.

The Ryans have split up. I tried to buy
the cabin from him, but he sold it to
a logging firm. At first I guessed he left
to be with you. I hardly knew her, yet
she wrote to me to say that she left him.

Her letter seemed to have a cedar smell;
I wished it came from you. The human brain
distinguishes among six basic odors:
putrid, fragrant, spicy, burnt, ethereal

and resinous. Hunger, humidity,
a woman's cycle of the month, and fear,
sharpen the sense of smell; migrating fish,
locating the first stream they swam by smell,
return where they were spawned; bees entering
a foreign hive are killed because the wrong,
betraying scent of their clan clings to them;
a female moth in heat attracts more than
a hundred males in half a day; if she
released the whole supply of bombykol
contained inside her sack in just one spray—
which she would never do—a million males
would gather to her in a single hour.

     Tonight I lecture here on moths. We are
all creatures, everything we do is willed
by what our species signals us to do—
even making believe. Before I sleep,
I sniff the forest in the cedar branch
I keep under the lamp beside my bed,
and then I dream I'm on that shell-strewn shore,
watching as you approach, pushing your way
out of the weedy lake, brushing hair from
your lips to ask who called you back. You see,
I understand why you pretend my name
has slipped your mind; you need to know me deeper
than my name can say. You must have smelled
the fragrant cedar twig I always carry
with me everywhere I chance to go.

STILL ON MY WAY

So I'll continue on my way, with your
good company, whoever you may be;
you'll get to know some of my other selves,
my cat, my dog, my monkey, my tame bear—
a yarmulke upon his comely head,
which he has grown accustomed to by now.
Now let's imagine that you are my twin,
since, when one gets right down to it, there's little
to distinguish us (yet maybe that's
enough to cause much harm) and that includes
the animals; we eat, we shit, we make love,
suffer, and we die. And let's assume
that we are walking by a silver stream
in autumn when the modulating leaves,
though still abundant on the trees, display
extravagance so sumptuous that we
receive their colors almost as a gift,
almost as if they flourished toward their end
as compensation for our being here.
My tame bear throws his shiny yarmulke
high in the whistling air to celebrate
his victory over his creaturehood,
though you, dear twin, may well suspect him for
some irreligious irony, despite
his rapt attention to the mystic way
the mellow colors merge and flair when touched
with intermittent light as a mild breeze
uplifts the nestled leaves and stirs the stream.
But then a huge wind that's accompanied
by rain so thick that it obliterates
the cringing sky and floods the shore, raises
a wave that stirs to mud the riverbank
and of the muck creates a monster from

the sunken past, a beast whose face takes on
the features of whomever it devours:
a cat, a dog, a monkey, or a bear,
and even you when terror twists your mouth
into a mask I hardly recognize.
　　　I see his smoky eyes pursuing you,
my twin, and then I see you disappear
into the forest mist. I hear a pause,
whose blank duration I can't estimate,
before the mist evaporates and lets
the blazing disk of orange sun return
into the unobstructed sky; then I
am back where I had been before the storm
descended like an angry god, and, lo!,
I see the spinning yarmulke float down
and land on the bear's head where it belongs.
　　　I'm pretty sure that I've recorded this
as it occurred, although I may have left
some details out since memories are not
infallible and get mixed up with dreams.
Ah yes, I now recall (though maybe longing
is a factor here) the monkey snatched
away the yarmulke and climbed a tree,
and—someone who had not been there to watch
might find what happened next incredible—
the monkey spoke. He said: "I sure enjoy
your company, although I didn't know
at first whom I could trust, and I'm amazed
by human laughter, how it can reveal
and make incarnate longing to connect,
to bind what chance and time would separate,
that drives you and your brother on your way."

GRIZZLY EXPERIENCE

Yes, I believe you when you tell me that
you have concern for my immortal soul;
you want to know how I can possibly
face death, death lasting for eternity,
with no faint expectation, not the slightest
tinge of hope, in any kind afterlife.
Here's why: during my recent surgery
my heart stopped for a second; when I woke,
there on my chest I saw the raw round circle
where the doctor zapped me back to life
with an electric shock. I'd seen no light
serenely, softly beckoning to me
when for that instant I was dead, nor did
I hear a Bach chorale to welcome me
to a more peaceful realm. But I'll recount
my most miraculous experience:
when hiking up a path in Glacier Park,
adding a white-winged crossbill to my list,
I was astonished when a bear lunged out
from right behind a huckleberry bush;
he stood immense on his hind feet as I,
without intent, blurted "Oh God!" out loud.
The stream I walked beside had ceased to flow,
the leaves on the grey aspens went stone still,
dark clouds turned luminescent in dark sky,
three ravens stood transfixed on one stiff bough,
and in that instant's stillness God appeared.
"You atheists are all alike," God said,
"when trouble comes you call on me for help,
but I don't mind, it's just what I expect."
I was chagrined, of course, and didn't want
to disavow my skeptical beliefs,
but God continued soothingly: "Here's what

I'm going to do" he said in his base voice,
"I'll turn this bear into a Christian bear,"
and pointing with his finger as immortal
Michelangelo depicted him,
the grizzly clasped his mighty paws together
in the gesture of a holy prayer,
and—this, I fear, may strain credulity—
the creature spoke distinctly as you hear
me speaking now. I never will forget
his piety: "Oh, Lord," said he, "I want
to thank You for this meal I'll now receive
as blessing from the bounty of Your hands."

    But as the bear was looking heavenward,
I bolted with more speed I'd ever dreamed
my legs possessed, and scuttled down the path
with cuts and bruises on my shins,
the scene behind me just a blur, the clouds
reshaping in the sky, and that's why I
agreed to meet you here, my friend, beneath
this ancient tree, to give some explanation
to the question you so kindly asked.

RABBI TO BUDDHIST PAL

"Oy weh! Oy weh!" My mother liked the sound
those groaned words made, so how can I discourse
on human suffering, when Jewish jokes
keep popping up unbidden in my mind?
But you instruct me with "Breath in! Breath out!
Renounce all acquisitions and desires;
never attribute blame, never take sides."
    A sudden whim compels me to reply:
"How can one run a business, choose a wife,
with such unworldly principles?" You nod,
my friend; you are not phased by my
defensive sassiness, although I think
that I detect some effort on your part
to hold back laughter at my quips. Humor
will always trump somber philosophy;
humor reminds us what we really are:
just animated clay, proteins, with lots
of water molecules. Those facts may not
be funny in themselves, but it is safe
to say they undercut pretentiousness,
releasing laughter to relieve the gloom
of sorrows we can't otherwise escape.
    But you advise me just to let my mind
float out like that laced solitary cloud,
streaked with a crease of evening light;
you say I should assume the quietude
that comes upon a wooded glen after
a thunderstorm, as if in listening
I might be anyone at all, thus free
of hurtful circumstance and chance.
    I hear my long-dead mother interrupt;
she says, "Show confidence whether or not
you're making sense. Chutzpah is what we learn

from God who's always breaking his own rules."
And then, a great grin spreading on her face,
she adds "If Buddha claims there is no self,
then whose arthritis is this in my bones?"
        Surely, you are amused by how
my mother's ghost remains my comic Muse;
I do not know what's really in your mind,
but I'm annoyed that you're not laughing at
my mother's joke. I still can hear
her parody of you: "Be here now and
then later you'll be somewhere else."
Perhaps she's right that wisdom masks nonsense
and makes it seem that it's profundity.

        But you reply I need to rid my mind
of memories, my mother's high-heeled stride,
her sweet tooth—"kuchen" was the word she used—
and the sharp pain that shocked her back and knees
right to the very end. "Okay," says I,
"I'll make a list, a catalog of all known things
I must remember to forget." And then, to my
astonishment, wild laughter seizes you,
so far beyond our empathy as friends,
beyond contending ideologies,
I wonder what you find so funny that
I must somehow have failed to laugh about.

        You look out and you point to that lone cloud—
I think I see what you must see—for, yes,
there is my mother robed in flowing white,
a golden harp held loosely at her breast,
strumming with fingers in a graceful blur,
strutting her stuff on the horizon's rim.

MUSE TO NEOPHYTE POET

    No detail is beneath attending to
in the pursuit of credibility,
so write about some real experience,
like lust or love, mundane as that might be,
but improvise when some embellishment
is needed to evoke what's possible:
things never are exactly as they are.
    Remember when you were just twelve years old,
your Grandpa had a reputation as
a lady's man; he liked to watch ripe women
from his beach chair by the local lake,
a stroll away from the red rented house
where you all gathered for the summer months.
One sunny day when swimming in the lake,
Grandpa sneezed forth a mighty sneeze that blew
his gleaming dentures from his startled mouth;
they popped right out and sank ten feet into
the weedy muck below. Word quickly spread
and titillated the community
and since it was well known that you excelled
at swimming, you were asked to put your mask
and flippers on and see if you could find
your Grandpa's teeth. The afternoon went by,
and still no luck, but then at misting dusk,
so legend grew, a dunking lady shrieked
she had been bitten by your Grandpa's teeth.
    Throughout the summer women swore that they
had been attacked; one lady had what looked
like bite-marks on her thigh, and threatened
to bring legal charges of assault. Grandpa
enjoyed his reputation as a flirt,
but now the joke was dangerous. And this
is where the question of credulity

is inescapable, and where my role
as your advising muse comes into play.

Here are some possibilities: Grandpa
gets sentenced to a one-year term in jail,
Grandma divorces him, the family is left
distraught in disarray—or else, perhaps,
the bitten lady who has brought the charge
against your Grandpa is in tight cahoots
with other ladies in the neighborhood
whose salty wish is to prolong the joke.

That's credible, consistent with the spirit
of your poem, so have the lady drop
her charge. Grandpa pretends he's not amused,
that his intentions have been falsified,
and when the buoyant ladies of the beach
appear with purplish bite-marks on their thighs,
Grandpa convenes a high-stakes poker game
and stays out with his pals till dawn comes up,
enjoying their complaints that women are
dissemblers who make too much of enough.

Perhaps you'll want your readers to believe
that you found Grandpa's teeth down in the slime,
the realm of flashing pike and pickerel,
but lied because the ladies would have been
denied a playful amorous repast
without those grinning, predatory teeth
lurking in those green depths; maybe you should
confess to lying just to win their trust,
or maybe your best strategy is that
you lie about your lying as your Grandpa
might have done when love was palpable
with lust's aroma in the summer air.

AUTHOR TO PROTAGONIST

      Out from the old stone fire-place, the bat
emerged into the room, circled about
in its erratic flight, and disappeared
as quickly as it had arrived; that scene
is where I want you to be recognized.
      My motive in creating you? I planned
that you'd become yourself, take on a life
that you could call your own within the plot
imagination has contrived for you—
a plot in which you're lost at sea, and while
you're gone, your father (think of him as me)
composes his own book about his son
who's able to enjoy a simple life,
such basic pleasures as just walking by
a sky-reflecting lake and listening
to loon calls echo from surrounding cliffs.
      The son has learned to watch the swirling clouds
absorb the orange evening light as if
clouds take delight in random shapes and shades,
the silhouettes of passing birds. AS IF—
his son (that's you, of course) can think in bold
conjectures so that what he is includes
the wishes he will have for his own son,
a singer with a silver voice, and also
gratitude to me as author and
as father who has placed transcendent music
in the reaches of his AS IF mind.
      And yet my ache to have real love returned,
real love from a real son, a pulsing ache
that's represented by the circling bat,
does it require that I depict you with
suspicion for your probing father, since,
like all of us, he too desires to be

more caring than in fact we are? Good will
may be my most redeeming attribute
or just the temporary respite from
my own raw, self-regarding restlessness,
envisioning a son who sees himself
from the perspective of his father's eyes
and seeks for freedom setting out to sea.
      Yes, that's the destiny I've given you.
Perhaps my author's agitation goes
way back to some lost prehistoric shift
in what we were as hunter-gatherers
mistrustful of each other's appetites—
a crucial shift that helped us to survive
by giving us the strange ability
to guess what's hidden in each other's minds;
a gift that grew to a grotesque excess
became the watchfulness haunting our dreams.
And so I try to think what you are thinking
your own wishful father thinks while you
are fabulously far away at sea.
      Out from some fetid bat-infested cave
with screeches echoing along cold walls,
your wordless ancestor uncertainly
steps forth, and, wary by a loon-spooked lake,
surmising how slant light contrives the cliffs,
conceives what he can barely recognize—
an image of himself outside himself,
watching as if he were his father who
watches his questing son set sail into
the legendary story of his life
to learn what his own unspent body can
and cannot do when trying to reach out
to feel the longing someone else might feel.

So what revision still remains for you
to make my inner life as rich as yours,
despite the fact that I exist only
as words appearing on this page—a scene
in which we're walking by a misty lake
with you depicted as my father, me
most likely reinvented as your son.

You've filled the father's mind with memories—
flashes selected no doubt from your life:
snow drifting or uplifted by the wind,
one crystal for a focused moment perfect
on your hand, cold turning warm—a warmth
that I can feel through your experience.

You have contrived me as your son with whom
the father seeks to reconcile—the son
who's run off with the wife of an old friend
from some dark need to cause him injury—
a mystery for me to ponder on.

I can refer to books you've had me read
to make my mind a meditative mind
like yours that values laughter more than all
the other-worldly remedies for grief—
as in that earth-bound poem when Hector's son
is frightened by his helmet and its plume,
and both he and Adromache break out
in open laughter even though both know
that Hector's death is imminent. This is
the laughter that my story hinges on.

That's why you have me conjure up King Lear
when with his faithful daughter, captured by
the enemy, they're being led to jail
and Lear, enraptured, claims they'll sing and "laugh
at gilded butterflies." I'm moved to see

how Lear is able to transcend his fate
by virtue of a fiction he conceives
with laughter on his elevated lips.
      But this is not what happens in the story
you've composed for me, in which your death—
I mean the character who stands for you
and gets shot in a petty robbery—
discloses no relationship between
your innermost identity at heart
and the chance circumstance of random death;
he never finds an opportunity
to comfort me for pain I've caused in my
inscrutable betrayal of a friend.
      Confession may well be your goal, although
your story's sticking point is pointlessness;
is that the insight you've awarded me?
What an absurdist I've become with guilt
you've laid upon my burdened life! Yet if
truly it were my option whom to choose
to tell my story, I am sure I'd still
have chosen you: a son must choose the father
of necessity who authored him.
      You've left me sitting here beside a lake,
just waiting for my story to resolve
its themes with some abstract formality—
a kind of soothing music of its own—
determined by its own internal laws.
      But I have one request—one last revision
to conclude my fabled life. Show me
reclining in pale morning light; show me
surrounded by vibrating lake reflections
shimmering hushed willow trees, where, now,
for the eternity you've given me,
I'm laughing at a gilded butterfly.

II

PAINTER TO SELF-PORTRAIT

With quick, repeating lines, pine needles bristle
into sight; a greenish smudge becomes
the trees' scent of voluptuous shade. Across
the valley, purple covers blue, the self-same colors
shadowing your eyes as you sit, watching
from a rock, the taste of blueberries
still on your lips. A northern, gray wind blusters
through with sliding shades, reminding you
your wife has gone to live with someone else—
his thick jaw, his uneven ears! Perhaps
the same wind darkened in the firs the time
your mother left your father for a man
who lived in Tucson, saddened in a week
because it didn't rain, and she returned.
    His portrait of her shows her naked, pale
to the waist, folding her arms beneath her breasts
to lift their circles to the rubbing light,
between two giant saguaros, both in bloom.
As if reflected on a lake, a coyote
curls within the throbbing cactus shade;
a silhouetted figure, halfway towards
the mountains maybe twenty miles away,
stares above the ragged tree-line at
the orange rock. Her diary may have
combined two stories since, before your birth,
your father left a desert girl to join
your mother who was waiting in Vermont.
He painted her in soft, receding snow-light
beside a waterfall descending from
the painting's edge, her hat pulled to her eyes,
remembering a former lover's hands.
    Perhaps you'll find, within the blues
emerging from the mountain mist, the reason why

your mother left him as he rested, gazing
by the window, where a nuthatch pecked
an icicle, recalling how the wind
wove through the August aspen leaves, flashing
their undersides, and scared the nesting grouse.
The first night she was gone, after her flight,
the swelling sun released its heat, making
the desert mountains bronze; her lips were dry;
they hurt her when she kissed him hard until
her body drew her into sleep. Your mother
never called him by his name, though she
described the golden fleckings of his eyes.
"The fear of loss," she wrote, "becomes a space
we fill with fantasies, a windy space
that separates our lives from where we live:
the lizard on his stone, his throat puffed out;
the leaping doe across a sloping field."
        Just like your mother, your wife will return.
As fox cubs bark beside their den, I'll set
the mountain range at dusk in darkest blues
and place your children in the windy woods
beside the waterfall; it will be March,
and she is walking at the field's north edge—
a stone wall piled a hundred years ago—
calling to them, "Come home!" too far away
to see your face, too far away to know
who waits for her upon a purple rock,
if it is you or just some trick of light.

The first thing that one notices before
one even sees your face, is the protruding
paintbrush ready to add on a touch
of thickest red in order to complete
the canvas world in which I am to dwell
in the similitude of permanence.

    Though you have fabricated me, we're not
identical, strange though that seems from where
I stare back at your staring gaze. You've chosen
to leave part of me unseen beneath
the varnished table top by which I sit
where it reflects the window in the wall;
some things I'll never know about myself.

    A woman's at the window looking in,
and in the hazy distance there's a stream
between two shaded hills receding to
what one might take to be infinitude.
Above the hills one barely can discern
black flecks suggesting crows. I don't know why
you've placed my lower half beneath the table
out of sight as if no clues about
my innermost identity were there
to be revealed; maybe you wished to hint
there's something private about each of us
that's better, kinder to leave unexplored.

    In full view of the would-be onlooker
my right hand reaches for the ripest peach
that rests in a ceramic bowl, or else
it seeks to nudge the paintbrush to the left
for some revision my hand has in mind—
if I might thus express an inclination
to equivocate from redder hues
to shadowed purples and to bluish greens,
lurking at the elusive edge of thought.

So what then am I thinking of? My face
shows only creases you can see, though I know
that you know I know something troubles me,
something about the face that's looking in
the window whom I almost recognize;
could that face be my mother's or my wife's?
She seems to focus on the dark beneath
the light the table gives back to the room.

Perhaps within that dark I'm wearing shoes—
the muddy working shoes I put on when
I'm gardening, or, if my feet are bare,
moon white with bluish veins, she notices
my twisted toes look like homunculi;
maybe that's why you've hidden them from sight,
though you can't stop such ghostly feet appearing
as hallucinations in your mind.

I wonder now if that bright bowl of fruit
on the square table top might be arranged
just as it once was long ago by my
departed mother, maybe by my wife,
and that you painted it from memory—
well, not exactly memory that you
can call your own, unimprovised, but what
you might attribute to me when in need
for some uncertainty to settle on—
uncertainty in blue or red or green.

GRANDPA RECALLED

I know you like to play the slot machines—
like hoping there's an afterlife; maybe
gambling is in our family genes, my son,
so here's some history to pass along
someday to your own son. Please don't assume
I've made this story up to justify
the chance I took in having you, the chance
my banker father took in having me.
　　The morning air was clear, bold chickadees
and sparrows squawked within the sycamores,
and I decided that I'd take a drive
to visit Grandpa just an hour upstate
where he spent August at a home for frail
but not demented folk. By then he had gone
almost blind, and after I arrived, his friends
took me aside and told me that he was
by far the most accomplished poker player
of the residents, and did I know
the secret of his spooky power to bluff.
　　Later, when by ourselves, I questioned what
psychology he used to win at cards,
and I can still hear his reply: since he
really could not tell what was in his hand,
he just assumed the best—a full house or
a high straight or a flush—and that was all
it took to win the pot. I drove back home
along a rutted, unfamiliar road
while wondering if he had improvised
a joshing explanation for my sake.
　　Next summer when I visited again,
his sight had gotten worse; he told me that
he had to give up playing cards, but that,
in compensation, he had been rewarded

with the gift of prophecy. "Like what?" I asked,
suspicious of the sly smile on his lips,
and he replied he'd had a vision how
this drifting world would meet its end
according to God's rolling of the dice:
"A wind comes off the ocean and I see
billions of seagulls tumbling through the sky
which closes on us with their panicked cries."

    I asked him, "Grandpa, what's the meaning of
God rolling dice, and when will He decide
our fate?" "It might be on the day I die,"
said Grandpa gravely, then his face lit up
as if his sight returned, "or on the day
you win a giant pot with a great bluff—
not with a royal flush against the odds
that there's a payoff in an afterlife
to calculate and safely bank upon."

    That's what your great grandfather said, my son,
it was the best joke he could pass along,
but if you're skeptical, let's make a bet
whether or not I made this story up
in his behalf; it's certain he would like
a God who takes His chances, rolling dice,
he'd like the stark, apocalyptic gulls.
By all that's holy in the universe,
I promise solemnly to tell the truth.

GRANDMA RECALLED

At my first Passover, Grandma proclaimed,
"My matzo balls are able to defy
the law of gravity, so eat them now
or else they'll float right off your plate. Last year
some stuck inside the chandelier—I had
to get a ladder from my neighbor's yard
so I could reach that high and scrape them off.
My recipe's a miracle—maybe
not equal to the Red Sea's parting so
we Jews could leave behind the yoke of our
Egyptian servitude, but it's a sign;
don't think God's not concerned with household things."

And now, my son, for your first Passover,
let me admit my childhood miracle
was that I gobbled down those matzo balls
and didn't die, although I still don't know
what purpose Yahweh spared me for, maybe
just to preserve important memories
that Grandma wanted me to share—like when
the Cossacks rode down from the roaring hills,
stole their fine jewelry and burned their homes.

They all escaped, bribing officials at
a border town, huddling and shivering
deep in an oceanic freighter's hold,
arriving in America where they
were free to buy and run a candy store—
a candy store—can you imagine that,
after what they had undergone, hiding
and sharing rationed portions of hard bread.

That's why you'll learn to eat your mother's
matzo balls tonight: to test your strength
for harder trials still to come—like those
inflicted by the Pharaoh in the past.

You're old enough right now to know
that there are people in the world that want
us all exterminated, blotted out;
that's how it is, that's how it was, that's how
forever it will be, unless Grandma,
busy as always up in paradise,
arranges for the Lord to intervene.

    The miracle of hers I liked the best
was that she made us laugh while lying there
right at the edge of death; I heard her tell
my mother she should have the windows washed,
since whether she recovered or did not,
there would be visitors parading through.

    Amused by her own joke, Grandma survived
for one more day, and when the neighbors came
to pay respects, there in the pantry stood
her matzo balls in rows of giant jars
ready to serve. And come indeed they did:
the baker brought us seeded rolls and cakes;
the grocer brought us carrots, beets, and greens;
the butcher brought us kosher sausages;
the mailman brought the paper with late news—
that Germany had just invaded France.
Did they teach you at school what happened next?

    I wonder now what Grandma knew up there
newly at home in distant paradise
with her adoring friends, how much bliss time—
eternity?—is needed to forget,
or can she still be cooking matzo balls?

It's been millennia since I have had
the potency to help or intervene
in your behalf, and rather than accepting
that sure fact, you've let yourself believe
your dark defeats and persecutions are
your fault, the consequence of failure to
uphold my laws, of disobedience.

    Not so. Blaming yourselves, you have evaded
the unthinkable: that I am not
omnipotent and can't protect you either
from your enemies or from yourselves.
Even in youth, I've been resentful with
a weakness for flamboyant gestures: floods,
and burning bushes, whirlwinds, thunder, plagues,
and smiting enemies. Yet records show
I've made some speeches that won't easily
fade from collective memory: as when
I told that stutterer, my one true friend,
that I would "circumcise his heart," although—
and I can't tell you why—I punished him
too harshly for a trivial offense,
a technicality of how to bring forth
water from a rock with words, not with a rod.

    Cursing was a great gift of mine—gory
afflictions, grotesque pestilence, yet I
did overcome my worst obsessions with
the body's frailties when I proclaimed,
"And I will send a famine not of bread
and not of thirst, but of my presence and
my words," so all would understand the worst
of torments tear the spirit and the heart.

    And after all this troubled history
of love and hate, reward and punishment,

I have one last confession still to make—
although you might have guessed it when I first
declared that humankind would be designed
in my own image, "male and female He
created them," as it was written down
at the beginning of my holy text.

        And, yes, of course there had to be—despite
my minimizing her—a Mrs. Yahweh
for both sexes to reflect divinity.
When sadly I look back, I wish that I
had listened more when she forewarned me of
the stings of parenthood; I suffered
from excessive rage and jealousy.

        And yet my laws were good; I was my best
when I exhorted you to empathy
when you exploited the bedraggled poor
for just a pair of shoes; and I was right
to chastise you for infidelity,
to threaten in the city dogs would eat
your carcasses; that in the sheep-filled fields,
fowl from the stinking air would swoop down to
devour you, so you'd take heed to know
your precious sense of justice came from me.

        Ah well, that's all behind me now, but it
has not worked out to leave you to your own
devices and failed sympathies; I'm grieved
you've paid the price for my mistakes. Maybe
some other god will get it right next time;
maybe he'll look out at the tangled woods
and shining fields and be content with fish
and birds and animals; maybe he'll know
he can't make a kind world all by himself.

MRS. Y HAS HER SAY

     I have my own guilt for the sorry way
things have turned out. I should have been insistent
from the start—though he depended on
my doting praise—that he not make his love
for them contingent on their love for him.
He overemphasized obedience
in testing them—Adam and Abraham,
Moses and Job, showing himself as one
who is conflicted, contradictory,
though he'd deflect the charge of craziness
just by demanding they have faith in him.
What dissimulation! What an excuse!
When he lacked words that could explain
why justice on the earth would not prevail,
justice that any child can understand—
sparing the innocent from pain—he bluffed.
Belief without reason to believe
was what he asked, but any open mind
could see the worldly facts: famine, disease,
coercion, war. Was none of this his fault?
     I think dissimulation started with
the story he contrived that Eve was born
from Adam's rib when he was sound asleep,
that nature, violating rules he made,
can be reversed, and males assume the role
of motherhood. What motive drove him to
such lunacy? And, worse, he punished Eve
for her heroic wish to learn, as if the quest
for understanding should not be their goal.
Treated by him as if I had no part
from the beginning when chaotic seas
were separated from the barren earth,
light from the dark, why did I not put forth

my own account of how creation led
to more creation still, how hungry life
that needed fatherly approval, also
needed mine—a truth that his account
obscured, despite his first commandment they
be fruitful, multiply, and make their seed
abundant as clear stars that mark the sky
or grains of sand that settle on the shore?

    My story would have left them satisfied
with just the roundness of a ripened peach,
 with just a hint of fragrance in the air,
with stars just for their glittering, not as
symbolic promises; there would not be
the need to take dominion or subdue.

    Death would seem no more frightening than dust—
oblivion from which they came, free from
awareness of themselves, from consciousness,
the source of suffering for loss as if
loss were avoidable and not the essence
of what nature is—the green renewal
of decaying green: the grass, the ferns,
the bushes, the lush trees. The false idea
of human immortality was what
he cursed their longing with; thus summertime
became desire, an apple on a bough;
desire became the wish for some condition
other than their own. Now he and I
are left with our contending histories
we have eternity to tell—though my
abiding heart still reaches out to him
to find some purpose for our endless days.

PASSENGERS

Were you asleep? Didn't you hear the news—
the captain's bland announcement that we must
prepare to land in an emergency?
He didn't bother saying to stay calm
or that we needn't fear a terrorist.
Maybe we do, and I can picture him
with his dark eyes ablaze with righteousness.
        Make sure your seatbelt's buckled tight, lower
your head and put your pillow over it;
remember where the exit is and that
you'll need the life vest if we crash at sea.
I'll never understand what causes men
to be so violent, so wounded mad
in thinking they alone know what God thinks.
Still after all these years I can't explain
what seems like uncaused hatred in the world,
hatred bred somehow from the need to hate.
        You've got a crucifix around your throat,
so maybe now's the time for you to pray
that by some miracle we both get spared,
although advising bearded God has not
had much success that I would know about—
even His son remained unrescued and
abandoned in the end. Maybe you should
attempt imagining an afterlife
in which all humans live in harmony,
all animals are vegetarians,
though I can't find much solace in that dream.
        Here, take my hand, and let my memory
provide you with your own experience
of motherhood: my son, in his red hat,
would stomp out in the snow with Dizzy, his
white dog, to play a heated game of chase;

Dizzy would circle him, then charge and leap,
snatching the woven hat right off his head
as sudden as the improvising wind.
He'd throw the hat high in the air, and when
Alan plunged through humped drifts to get it back,
Dizzy would zoom right in and snatch the hat
I'd knitted for him as a birthday gift.
I still can seem him wildly shaking it,
holding it tightly in his mouth, Alan
pursuing him with laughing cries along
 the somersaulting hill—the hat a flag
proclaiming victory for nothing more
than creature happiness the body finds
in life itself, unmediated life.

     My son's a surgeon now; I'd like for you
to meet him if somehow we get through this.
Not all men harbor murder in their hearts
or know themselves only by knowing who
they must assume must be their enemy.
Hold tighter to my hand, just concentrate
on what I'm telling you, the frozen scene
of icicles and pines, a whirling dog
the color red against the background white,
and Alan's laughter misting in the air
as if he's shouting news from paradise.

TERROR IN ITS LAST LIGHT

   Don't tell me that we're in the hands of God;
we're going to crash because of engine failure
or a terrorist, and you're the one—
not someone whom I care about and love—
I'll have to spend my final moments with.
I was suspicious when you first sat down,
your fumbling with your shoes, unwillingness
to meet my eyes, but you're as innocent
as all the rest of us, so why should I
resent your sitting next to me? Maybe
I'd get to like you if I knew enough
about your life—your wife, your kids; maybe
we could be fishing buddies as I was
with my own brother till an argument
tore us apart. Incredibly, I can't
recall what it was that we fought about—
a fight with fists; I can't remember what
had set us at each other's throats. I know
as much about him now, as I know you.
   I still can see myself at misty dawn,
the backswing of my rod making an arc
which let my line swing out across the stream
and land exactly where a trout would hide.
Yes, I could read the minds of hungry fish,
but I can't understand how terrorists
learn so much hate—people they do not know—
that they could choose to die to feed that hate.
   Can hate just be some blind excuse for one
to kill oneself? I do not want to hear
about your faith in God. Tell me about
your brother whether he exists or not;
make him an even combination of
your father and a friend. Quickly, be quick,

this moment matters though it is our last—
alive we're still alive, eternity
is now. I'll picture you beside your brother
by a waterfall above a pool
made up of mossy rocks; its spume reflects
a little rainbow arc: the pool is filled
with red and yellow leaves although the trees
are not yet bare. A looming orange sun
suffuses a swirled cloud, which instantly
reminds me of a face with down-turned lips
 prepared to fill the shocked sky with a scream—
a face I almost recognize, although
its features could belong to anyone.

CLIENT TO LAWYER

Maybe you won't believe me, and perhaps
it's better some uncertainty remains
so you'll defend me with a woman's zeal;
I swear to you I didn't rape that girl.
Not only did I have consent, but I
was certain that she loved me—just as I
believed with all my heart that I loved her.

I just can't understand how I could be
mistaken in my judgment that we shared
desire, shared the very wish to share.
How could I fail to comprehend that she
might have had divided feelings because
we each have been brought up in different faiths.

The place it happened? By a lake, haunted
by loons, reflecting orange lantern lights
from a pavilion where slow dancers swayed
to sentimental music from the past;
the scented air was soft and the full moon
defined the features of her perfect face.
I felt swept up in the whole history
of human love, from when it first evolved
out of blind body urges and then merged
with ideals of fidelity and trust.

Strange as it sounds, I must confess I think
the devil had a hand in this, that my
confusion did not have its origin
entirely in me; don't get me wrong,
it's not that I equate his influence
with lust, or anything deliberate—
the wish to dominate—but rather that
he must have clouded my intelligence,
preventing me from reading what was in
her deeper mind. You look incredulous,
but I'm not speaking just in metaphors,

I often think the devil's strategy—
convincing people he does not exist—
has been effective these last centuries.

     Some things cannot be logically explained;
how could I rape a girl I truly loved?
You are a little older than I am,
but you're attractive too; does beauty give
you power to see something in me that I
can't see? I think the devil has a hand
in all the sorrow beauty brings about
whose causes seem inscrutable to me.

     Her face was chiseled by the moonlight like
an alabaster statue with no blood;
the lake shone with the gleam of orange lights,
its surface undulating in the breeze:
I can't blot out these pictures from my mind.
And something tells me there's a message in
the water's rocking and the certainty
that nothing is exactly what it is.
So how can you defend me if I don't
know what to plead or what I'm guilty of?

LAWYER TO CLIENT

So why this Mr. X wants you released
or why he wants his true identify
unknown, evokes suspicion in a mind
trained to be skeptical like mine, but since
he has agreed to pay all legal fees,
my obligation only is to you,
and if you tell me you are innocent—
well, murder is no easy charge to prove,
especially the murder of a twin.

The fact there was confusion as to who
killed whom, and that you were the one police
first thought had been stabbed with a kitchen knife,
helps us in challenging the evidence
the prosecution will bring forth in court.
You'll testify you and your brother's wife
were now just friends, despite the troubling fact,
which you admit, you slept with her before
she married him. Something in nature seems
to make blood brothers amorously drawn
to the same woman—although everyone
will find her dangerously beautiful.

But who'll believe your story if you think
the devil played a part in this, that he's
the author of your jealousy—surely,
you are just testing my credulity.
As any doctor knows, this cannot be
an explanation we can use in court,
although some superstitious jurors might
consider that it makes God-fearing sense.

You must present yourself as if you are
an ordinary, decent guy, caught up
in complex tangles of appearances,
a surgeon known in the community,

for that's the best defense we have to mount.
And yet you still insist a chance exists
our unknown Mr. X might be the devil
in disguise, since buying souls is what
he's always done. But if that's really so,
what motive might he have to get you off?

      Do I sense a confession there? Are you
suggesting an insanity defense
is our best strategy? I grant you that
it's rare to find a man who can resist
the lure of female charm. I sympathize
and have a deceased brother of my own—
as surely you well knew in choosing me
to represent your case. And you know too
how gruesome I would find these stabbings, these
repeated stabbings in the eyes, as if
the killer did not want to witness what
he'd done, as if in blinding his twin brother, he
could blind himself, deny his jealousy
belonged to him. I shared much happiness
with my own brother when we fished together
in the dawn, although he had more luck
than I, and that grates in my memory
as if it happened yesterday. Tell me
the truth—you know I'll sympathize—did you
connive for Mr. X to hire me?

DEAR SEYMOUR PENN

For thirty years my wife and I have read
your books and wondered what you're like. Before
she married me, during the war, she loved
a man who has your name. He disappeared,
and all these years I've thought that you might be
the man she knew. Her photograph of him
looks like your last book-jacket pose, but he
was so much younger then, I can't be sure.
The picture is enclosed; you'll be amused,
for there he is—laughing, leaning against
a redwood gate beside a lemon grove,
his feathered hat in hand, and gesturing
for everybody to come in as if
to smell the ocean in the lemon trees.

My wife has been too shy to write herself,
and anyhow you know how women like
to fantasize; that's why I've always let
the matter pass. But when, in your last book,
I read a passage where a man like me—
unknown, mindful of others, getting old—
exactly in this circumstance, decides
to write and ask an author he admires:
"And have you ever loved my wife?" I felt
finally it was time to contact you.

I hope to learn if you're the man who knew
my wife, but since the author in your book
chooses not to reply—although it's clear
he has the aching need for reaching out—
I have no clues. So I've composed a scene
in which the author, fascinated by
the picture sent him by a man like me,
writes back to say: "Astonishing though it
may seem, the orchard keeper by the gate
could be my brother, lost at sea after

he bought a lemon grove; he planned to bring
his would-be wife out to the coast so they
could settle there." The picture makes him wish
he'd lived the life his brother might have lived—
each pungent day among the lemon trees—
and he decides he wants to write a book
about a couple married thirty years.
A bachelor, he makes a strange request;
he asks if he can visit us to learn.
"You'll hardly know I'm there," he promises,
but I can sense he sees my wife through his
lost brother's eyes; already he is half
in love with her, staring at the pulse beat
that startles like a sparrow in her neck.

     And that's the story's gist so far. But if
you want to know what happens next, then I
can send you more; even you, a master
plot-maker, will find yourself surprised.
I trust this bond of ours because I feel
us touching as I write—as palpably
as sunlight shimmering the lemon trees.
Beneath the blandness of most people's lives,
incredible things occur—like now, like this.
These thirty years—they are all frozen there
across a wall and through a redwood gate.

     In my own life, I've waited for your book
to tell me what to do. And now you have.
You knew the author in our book could not
explain himself, that I would have to write
his history. When I knew that you knew,
I smelled the ocean in the lemon trees
so powerfully, the salt stung on my lips.

     My wife sends her regards, and wonders if
you would believe her lover is my own
invention, that the picture here is me.

One life is not enough—or so it seems
with Hank, though we've been married twenty years.
I still can see him by the picket fence
his father made him paint each spring. "Hey there,
I have an extra brush, give me a hand!"
were his first words to me. He didn't seem
to notice that my hand was not quite right.
Not that he's been unfaithful; I believe
his shocked assurances are true. But he
admires your husband's novels so darn much,
his people (as Hank calls them) are so real
to Hank, that when he talks of them (a lot!)
I feel as if they're living in our house.

      Last night when I complained (I rarely do),
we argued half the night, and then I dreamed
I gave birth to a girl—your husband's child.
Today I broke a pitcher in the sink—
my mother's wedding gift—and I resolved
that I would write to you, though we first met
barely a month ago. We live almost
secluded by a lake surrounded with
old willow trees. I like my privacy;
most of my day is well spent tying quilts.
I am designing one right now with geese
migrating past a hazy sun, stroking
their wings in unison, each one assigned
to its own place. I'll send a photograph
when it's complete, and if it pleases you—
tell me your birthday. Virgo is my guess.

      In his last book, your husband's heroine
is crippled in an accident; only
her daughter goes on loving her. I wonder
if she's modeled after you. If so,

perhaps you'd like me to explain (I'll try)
how I have dealt with my infirmity.
Just let me blurt this out: your husband has
made people from some need to feel complete;
how can you tell you are not one of them?
How can you tell you're not invented too?
Hank needs me as a listener. He talks
about your husband's characters as if
they were his own, and gives them lives that change
the book: "If Jack had left Corinne . . ." and off
he goes where I have no desire to go.

    I feel I've never been alone with Hank.
(I've never caught him looking at my hand.)
He says I'm like our lake at dawn before
the wind's first stirring in the willow trees—
as if that were his final compliment.
My mother thinks that Hank's best feature is
his smile, and yet his cuspids are so large
they press against his upper lip. Maybe
this will amuse you: when I married him,
I dreamed I stole back to the picket fence
to paint the outermost two pickets black.
Hank's told this story now so many times,
he's come to think my dream is his. "Without
those teeth of mine," he'll say, "you never would
have married me; you would have married Bill."
And off he goes with me just listening.

    Men are like children in their needs. Did you
applaud your husband when his book was done?—
"Bravo! my darling, yes it's beautiful!"
Even if true (as in your husband's case),
there's something human such truth fails to touch.

    Before I send this letter off, I'll take
another walk around the lake to watch
the trees' reflections as the colors change:
the lake absorbs the blue-grays of the sky

and passes on a purple hue to tinge
the yellow willow leaves. (One can mistake
a cedar waxwing for a robin in
this light.) Then I'll be ready to decide
whether to sign this with a pseudonym
and see if you can guess that it is me.

BROTHERS

It's not that I expected you, and yet
the doctor says the news is pretty good;
they can't be certain that they got it all.
So does that mean I should prepare myself
to live or die? How can one make a joke
of that? I can remember Rabbi Gold
who ran the synagogue when we were boys:
the final years before he died, he suffered
from arthritis in his feet, although
his mind stayed clear; he'd start each welcomed day
with breathing exercises slow and deep,
and then he'd study his Talmudic texts
as was his practice all his life. But first
he offered up a simple prayer to God:
he thanked the Lord for His allowing him
to die from bottom up instead of from
top down, and that's the stoic model I
desire to emulate. The doctor said
just pretty good, but what if pretty good
by chance should turn to good, and what if good
got better and then somehow better turned
to best so I was cured, completely cured,
and then, miraculously, best of all,
my body started to grow young—nature
had found a way to have her processes
reversed and thus at last preserve herself.
        You ask why me? Well I say, why not me,
it's just a question of the odds, and if
some quantum lottery is going on,
someone must win; it's not unfair to say
I have deserving attributes: no one
enjoys a mountain vista more than I,
tasting the evening air like vintage wine,

or drifting down a river in the fall
along the shore-line where floating red leaves
make way as if they're welcoming my boat,
my journey nowhere in particular,
just wanting to be only where I am,
desiring only to remain myself.
　　　So I'm prepared to be the one nature
might wisely choose for her experiment
with permanence, as if she had enough
of change and wished at last to settle down
as you did with your wife and your three kids.
　　　Do you think this is all just top-down talk?
I can still see your eyes, your mocking face,
pretending to look glum and serious,
just as you humored me through all those years
when you were airy laughter and alive.

SISTERS

Maybe because she was so young, Dad's death
meant something to Nicole it didn't mean
to us—betrayal of her trusting love, as if
he didn't have to suffer that last stroke
and thus abandon her. To her all men
are bound to be unfaithful in the end,
and those she picked fulfilled what she most feared.
    I told her this each time she got divorced
and each time afterwards when an affair
ended in bitterness, but she could not
acknowledge her hostility; bad luck,
she thought, some people have bad luck in love.
    I know we share the same grim view of her,
despite our good advice that she should face
her fate with humor and should buy a dog,
so I'm both troubled and confused why you
had lunch alone with her last week without
your telling me. What could you say to her
or she to you that's not for me to know?
    I saw you in the restaurant, intent,
leaning as close as merging breaths could reach;
I wasn't there to spy, only to shop—
for lingerie in case you're curious—
and so I kept on walking down the street.
    What happened next was quite astonishing:
the block had been sealed off for a parade
with marching bands, high-stepping girls, and floats,
but bursting through the barrier, a horse,
its carriage still attached to it, without
its driver to direct where it should go,
careened along the street, so terrified
its eyes were widened and their whites, like moons—
as if I had been singled out—focused
on me for reasons past imagining.

A giant Donald Duck balloon escaped
its holders and ascended heavenward,
and though I felt I was in danger I
just couldn't help but laugh to think I'd witnessed
the transcendence of a duck. The horse
crashed wildly in the window of a store
that sells expensive jewelry—no doubt
that detail interests you—and then collapsed,
twitching and bleeding, helpless on its side,
the empty carriage still attached to it.
  A great illumination filled my mind:
we are not in control of our own lives;
such circumstances as our father's death
affect us in a realm where impulse rules,
where choice and will are impotent, and we
are most what we don't know about ourselves,
like ducks imprinted with their destiny.
  Now tell me everything you told Nicole.

Heather, three years have passed since we have all
been here, and it was raining that day too.
I'm sorry I insisted that you come;
I know you need to get away with Dave
before your baby's due—you ought to see
what someone's chiseled on the back side of
your father's stone. I'm not sure who it is,
although before your father died, he had
a client, Ben, a taciturn young man,
accused of bludgeoning a brother in
a drunken fight, but he convinced the jury
Ben was not the kind of man who murders
what he loves. Your father spoke with such
persuasive eloquence, I never won
a single heated argument with him.

Ben turned to sculpting when he was released;
perhaps he feels he's paying off a debt
by etching on the stone. See, there it is—
it must have taken months: the animals
in pairs, the ark beneath the risen sun,
with Noah and his wife waving goodbye,
though not one beast turns back for a last glimpse
of where it's been. Look at the care that's gone
into the etching of the lion's mane,
the knotted shag around the camel's ears!

Beth comes here by herself; she likes to be
alone with her own thoughts. She was the one
who first discovered that the stone was marked:
I never looked behind it when I placed
a cedar wreath upon his grave because
he didn't like cut flowers, though he knew
their names: bloodroot and toadshade, adder's tongue
and wet-dog trillium and spiderwort;

98

he would recite them like a witch's chant.

  Your sister worries me. Your father's death
still troubles her. The colored birds she paints
have such large eyes that look directly at you
from whatever branch or stump they're on.
I wonder what Beth thinks their wide eyes see.
The dove, she says, should not be carrying
an olive leaf; that's why the carver left
his work undone. Heather, it bothers her,
I'm sure, that you got married first, though she
is four years older than you are, and soon
you'll have a child. Beth hoards too many feelings
for herself—or for her staring birds.

  Did you know Audubon, meticulous
observer though he was, painted some birds
that no one else ever has seen—as if
he'd really watched them startled in the woods?
People need ways of making things their own.
Your father kept a life-list of wild flowers:
Heather was underlined—I noticed that,
cleaning his desk after he died, and I
imagined why he chose that name for you.

  I'll tell you what I think. I think that Beth
is seeing Ben, that she instructed him
to make engravings on the stone. Ben didn't
realize that flying from the ark
the dove would not have held an olive leaf,
so Beth decided that he stop his work.
And I suspect . . . Heather don't give me that
aggrieved, exasperated look of yours—
as if you think I've planned all this to get
you here to mourn your father as you should!

DISAPPEARANCE

I can't believe you don't remember whether
Grandma's eyes were brown like Jill's or gray
like mine! Dark gray—I'm almost certain, Mom,
that they were gray, set close against her nose.
You've always said I have her stubborn way
of seeing people as I wanted them,
while Jill was more remote and critical.
     Doesn't it scare you, Grandma's only dead
three years, and she's begun to blur. I see
her shuffling in the kitchen, never outside
in the sun, stirring her pot of stew,
sipping the spoon, with steam around her ears
as if she conjured her own autumn mist.
My clearest memory: she's scolding you—
her tightened hair in its eternal bun,
her breast puffed out like some endangered bird
that's summoning its brood—because you failed
to telephone Aunt Jenny on her birthday
as you promised Grandma that you would.
"Sisters have got to keep in touch," she said.
     You were offended by how Jenny dressed;
I heard you tell Dad that you didn't want
her in the house with her cheap rabbit fur
and her array of phony mink and fox,
but she would mimic you when she dropped by
and make Dad laugh so hard he'd snort and grunt.
I hated Dad's crude laughter; I was happy
Jenny moved away when Grandma died,
but I regret now I once felt that way.
     Before she disappeared, Jenny arrived
to talk to me, just me. I'd never seen
her wear so many furs: her hat, her coat,
her gloves, even her boots, and I almost

didn't recognize her with her eyebrows
penciled in black, her lips slicked shiny white,
talking so rapidly that little foam balls
bubbled at the corners of her mouth.
She frightened me, holding my wrists to make
me look directly in her face as she
informed me Grandma loved you more than her.
She spoke those words in whispers, tugged her hat,
and told me I was more like her than you.
 I don't know what connects these things, but when
you said you weren't sure if Grandma's eyes
were gray, Jenny's long face came back as if
a fox poked from its lair and stared at me
across the hillside through the windy snow.
Was Grandma as composed as she appeared?
I never heard her shout or saw her rush—
or has your memory lost hold there too?
 I'm good at hiding what I feel, that's why.
I half suspect Jenny wore furs to show
we all need some disguise, providing that
we don't disguise ourselves too perfectly.
She'd never told you where she went, although
I'll bet that she left Dad her number just
in case . . . She'll know if Grandma's eyes were gray!
If we forget one single hair of hers,
everything else from toe to fingertip
will follow down the light and slip away
like Jenny walking off that afternoon
into the shaded snow. She saw me watching
from the window when she doffed her hat.
Her eyes were gray like Grandma's, and like mine,
and maybe that's why you forgot, or why
you're wondering if Jill knows that I'm here.
 I bought this funny hat for you only
because it's been a cold and windy fall;
I had no premonition that we'd talk

of Jenny after all this time, trying
to bring her gray eyes back in memory,
trying to make her one of us again.

LEVIATHAN

You've kept your word and come to visit me.
You know how much I love this house, although
I'm lonely here. Your father used to walk
this beach with me, then sit on that smoothed rock—
as if the sea prepared a seat for him—
observing sails tack past the buoy bells,
waiting for a whale's spout to appear.
      It seemed he would forget how many times
he told me: when he was a boy, he took
his rowboat out to get a close look at
the baby whale that strayed into the bay.
Descending underneath your father's boat,
it surged up bubbling on the other side,
flipped around, dove beneath his boat again,
drenching your father with each salty plunge.
Circling beyond the reef, its parents flung
their thirty tons into the sky—with a
vast whoosh of blown-out sea, their plume of spray,
and then a hiss of air as if it sucked
the whole horizon in—displaying white
repeating patterns on their undersides,
pounding their tails to summon its return.
      Your father claimed it dove beneath his boat
at least a dozen times before it left,
but he regretted that he didn't leap
into the sea himself to play with it.
I'm still amazed to think how all his life
that rankled him, and yet that may have been
the most ecstatic day he ever spent.
"I swear the damn thing laughed at me," he'd say,
"its whistles, chirps and clicks composed a song."
      Your father thought he was a happy man,
but something willed about his happiness

showed through, something deliberate. I felt
he had to make a choice to hold gloom down.
And yet he couldn't bring himself to say
what troubled him; I don't know if he knew,
and never did find out. A certain blank,
distracted gaze would sweep across his face
when that grim mood of his came on, making
his eyes seem vague—the way a camera
blurs one's age lines when it's not in focus.
Sadness in him—if it is accurate
even to say that it was his—rarely
connected with particular events;
it simply would emerge and disappear
like hemlocks in the autumn morning mist,
and there was nothing I could do to help.
I had to live with it, so I assumed
that I was not the cause. Last night you spoke
to me in that remote, abstracted voice
your father sometimes used, when you remarked:
"There's just one man my wife would leave me for—
our son; it's like competing with a ghost."

     Your father used to praise me for the care
I'd given you and Jennifer, but not
the caring I showed him. I don't mean he
would blame me for his sorrow, yet I'm sure
he wished somehow I could have found a way
to lighten what he called the tears of things.
How could I? What he felt was much too deep
and too impersonal—like rain, or mist,
or snowfall in the oak's remaining leaves.
I fear he passed that sorrow on to you.
Yes, he was right about himself—sorrow
revealed the soul of things, especially
when they were beautiful; sorrow for him
was out there moving in the universe.

     Perhaps he loved the changes of the fall

too much: the orange maples, goldenrod
at the field's edge, and you, your muscled arms
just like his own. Before you left, you split
the last dry cord of wood for him. He leaned
against the window watching you, and when
you came inside—do you recall?—he told
his story of the baby humpback whale,
but with a change. I'd never heard before
that when the whales dive down and disappear,
they leave patches of oily water, almost
imperceptible and strangely still,
which look like human footprints on the sea.

GHOST STORY

I've found three people now who claim they've seen
the girl's ghost underneath the apple tree
where she last met her lover on the night
he strangled her. Sue is upset with me:
she says things need repair around the house;
a grown man shouldn't waste his time asking
about ghosts. You know, Mom, that I don't believe
in ghosts, but she's become a legend here;
her murder gave the farmers something besides
planting to talk about. As you'd expect,
the girl was beautiful—with straight, black hair
that caught the moonlight like a summer lake;
astonished, dark-brown eyes; and skin so pale
some people wondered if she might be ill.
But no one could describe the boy, except
he lisped. The girl was pregnant when she died,
and everyone is sure he murdered her,
although he disappeared from town without
a fingerprint to make quite certain he
was there that night. Her being pregnant doesn't
seem to me sufficient proof, and yet
it's also said the boy refused to help
his father with the milking chores. Three nights
I hid behind the old, stone orchard wall
to watch the apple tree, not expecting
truly to see her ghost, yet trying to
imagine her exactly as she stood
there waiting for her lover to appear.
The third night someone came—a man, I'd say
about my height and build, and carrying
a stick or rifle, maybe hunting for
raccoons, or else her sleepless father might
have wandered through the orchard wishing to

out-walk his grief. I called to him. At first,
as if expecting me, he looked around,
then ran across the orchard to the woods.
Sue says I'm lucky that he didn't shoot.

      Sue doesn't know I've come to talk to you.
The difference between Dad's books and what
the farmers saw is only that Dad knows
his characters exist as words. Explain
to Sue all his inventions are just ghosts!
And yet I wanted Sue to understand
the real fear that girl felt. Picture her face!—
that's what I should have said—surely someone
might have perceived the danger she was in,
and tried to rescue her. That's what her father
should have done—or else some neighbor's boy
who loved her, though she had rejected him.
And if I write her history, at least
her memory will live—if not her child.

      I'll get the details right—the scudding clouds,
the apple trees in rows, a piled stone wall,
the lacy, sleeveless dress that showed her arms.
But whom should I include—her father, Sue,
both you and Dad, a neighbor's boy, myself?
Sue's almost got to see her underneath
the apple tree in August moonlight, fear
on her hushed face, the shaded flowing
of her silver arms, a cameo around
her thin, tense throat, maybe just like the one
you always wear, engraved with circling birds,
that has my tinted portrait tucked inside.

SPACES

Dad, you can work the Skil-saw while we talk,
then let me have my turn to finish up.
I need to borrow money. My old friend,
Teddy, offered me the chance to buy
into his firm, designing private homes.
Be careful, watch the blade! I've talked to Mom;
she loves the house Teddy built for his Dad—
the picture windows and the cave-like rooms,
so that close space flows outward to the field
and gathers where the willows frame the lake.

A house should be an image of the mind—
it should invoke the feelings people need
that don't exist until there is a form
to hold them in. Mom said you might not let
me pay you back; I know that in the deepest sense,
I can't, but something I can pass along
I've learned from you will grace each house I'll build:
of balances, of lines repeating and
of forces that connect. Mom says she's saved
some money just for me; she thought it might
be better if I used her money so
I'd feel that I was starting on my own.

Mom said her mother left it all in trust
to use when the time came. I must have been
about thirteen when Grandpa cut those oaks
to use as barn-beams; Grandma hardly talked
to him for days. "They'll all grow back," he said,
but Grandma told me that he could have bought
them somewhere else. I think I understood
how people love things in their different ways.
Pausing to sniff the wood, Grandpa whittled
it like a sculptor; he'd close his eyes
and rock his head as if in holy prayer.

Maybe I could borrow half the money
from you and half from Mom. But Dad, you've got
to let me pay you back. If you insist,
put it in trust and save it for my son.
You're always getting wood-chips in your eyes.
You rest, I'll work the saw a while. Teddy
has a commission for a house right now
he wants me to design—it's just my kind
of landscape with a view along a row
of pines and cedars leading to a lake.
I told Mom that I'd like to have the roof
slope upward from the west to east; I want
a feeling of the flow of space outward
past trees and lake and, if the night is clear,
into the constellation of the stars.

      You're going to hurt yourself today! I'll cut
those last few boards while you clean up.
I shouldn't give away my strategy,
but Mom suggested that I talk to you
while you were sawing wood. I've never kept
secrets from you; I know you see through me
too easily. There goes that grin of yours;
you're worse than me at keeping feelings in.
Promise that you will let me pay you back.
I'd like to build a house for you someday,
but you won't move from here. We both know that,
though Teddy told me that his parents felt
the same way once, and I'll admit, Mom guessed
I could persuade you if I timed it right
with all the scented wood-dust in the air.

      That grin of yours is more suspicious than
I thought at first. Tell me the truth, come on,
where did Mom get the money? It's my hunch
you figured that I'd be either stubborn,
like knots that break the rhythm of the grain,
or too proud and refuse to ask for it.

But you're so full of mischief and surprise;
I think she may have gotten it from you.

GOING AND STAYING

The first time that your mother flew to see
her father when he had a stroke, I dreamed
she almost crashed, and when she flew again,
the dream returned. I watched her climb the stairs,
then turn and wave. Her lips called "Stay in touch!"
although she couldn't spot me in the crowd;
and then I saw her calves, her purple shoes,
the sun's glare on a wing as if it were
a windless bay, and then the dark inside.
    A man with outstretched geese embroidered on
his shiny tie—whose face I couldn't quite
make out—sat next to her, and when the dark
blinked smoky red, he drew her to his chest.
A wing exploded, pivoting the plane;
I woke before it hit the ground, angry
at her, and asked her not to fly that day.
If there's a wish contained in such a dream,
my son, it's not the wish I chose to wish.
    That night we held each other, and the fear
drained from my body, but I dreamed again—
again she climbed the windy stairs, the sun
gleamed on a wing, the old man's blue-veined hands
fondled her sunken head. The burning plane
spun earthward as his features changed—I woke
when his flushed face squeezed to an infant's cry.
    Still half asleep at breakfast, I could see
wild geese migrating through the surging mist;
I pleaded that she wait another day.
But when she left this house we built together
and the apple orchard that we tended with
the drunken bees, I saw her silent lips
say "Stay in touch!" as if somehow she knew
when she arrived, her father would be dead.

Look how the mist recedes! One cannot tell
exactly where the snow-capped mountains end
and where the clouds begin; even the pines
seem shadows that the clouds cast on the wind.
    I haven't had that dream again, but when
I hear the misted geese, those images
return—red darkness, and the man, grown back
into a child, touching her cheek. After
her father's funeral, when she came home,
I thought you noticed that we did not kiss.
You said you'd never want to fly. And yet
it's beautiful up there—distance does that,
and I'm afraid loss does that too. The wheat,
the harrowed earth, the tassled, gleaming corn,
seem painted only for the color's sake.
    But if I dream tonight, maybe I'll see
her final "Stay in touch!" parting her lips.
She'll gaze outside to hear the apple blossoms
humming with the bees and watch the colors
of the landscape stream away below—
as if those words were meant for everyone.

PERSUASION

You want to marry Jane—my daughter Jane?
For God's sake, Bill, you and Nancy drove me
to the hospital when she was born!
You said that I was blessed to have a girl.
You've been my closest friend for twenty years!
Each New Year's day till Nancy died, you helped
Jane dress her snowman in your ear-muff hat;
you would confide to it through your cupped gloves:
"Now you don't have to listen to the wind!"
    The camping trip we took that spring before
Nancy had her stroke, when Jane slipped crossing
a stream and sprained her knee; you lifted her
up on your shoulders, but she cried for me
to carry her. You sulked the whole way home
as Nancy teased you: "Every woodsman needs
a daughter of his own!" Her laugh cascaded
like a waterfall—until the stroke
twisted her eyes; her mouth drooped to a scowl.
I wondered if her illness angered you
and changed the way you treated her, although
you told me at her funeral you thought
you couldn't love again. A hailstorm tore
the apple skins the day she died—winter
in the blazing midst of summertime, I thought—
and I remember that you said: "At my age
friendship is enough reward for me."
    And now you want to marry Jane! I know
that friends can be replaced—that hurts, but not
what hurts the most; Jane's age hurts even more.
Did you know that my mother was in mourning
when we met on that canoeing trip?
You sat upon a boulder by the shore,
and as I landed my canoe, you put

a finger to your lips to quiet me
so you could hear the early loons reply
across the water where the wind had dropped.
The ôô in loon brings back my father's voice,
mellow and distant, yet for all the times
we've listened to the loons call by a lake,
I never told you how my father died.

       Though he was forty when he married her,
each anniversary they'd pack a tent
and climb Mount Marcy's steepest trail; I think
he died while they were making love. My sister
still resents his death and hasn't found
a man to marry yet. Spring love is for
putting in the seeds; summer is for tending;
fall is for gathering and letting go.
It's not too cold yet, Bill. Let's spend a week
canoeing on the Allagash. We'll fish
and listen to the water lull the shore,
letting our voices drift across the lake
until we hear our echoes in the pines
sigh and fade out in the receding wind.
And you'll forget. Nancy would want you to.
I still can see her laugh at what she called
our "woodland ritual," her forehead veins
blue as a rivulet, her eyes just like
my father's—ice gray flecked with gold. The loons,
the soothing loons will help you to forget.

INCURABLE

Maybe I've had a prejudice against
surgeons since my mother's operation,
but I believe you're trained not to respond
to suffering; that's why I disapprove
of Margaret's marrying you. I'm sure you think
I'm not prepared to let my daughter go,
but I am still convinced surgeons must learn
how not to grieve. Look at you now—there's not
a ripple on your face to show you don't
like what I've said. You're taught to think of flesh
by feeling with a knife—as if the line
dividing cruelty from cure were drawn
so fine, only a steady hand, and not
the blundering, brave heart, could trust itself.

    I brought you here, this meal's on me, so have
the sirloin steak, the mushroom sauce is done
exactly right. After my mother's stroke,
they cut the left side of her neck to clear
the blocked-up artery and get more blood
into her brain. I watched for one whole week;
her speech returned, she could remember me.
But then another blood-clot formed; her chin
dropped to her chest, she drooled, baby sound "ôô"s
bubbled upon her tongue. The surgeon said
"We'll go in on the right" as if there were
some hidden life reserved inside her head
that he alone could find. He had the look
your eyes have now when he said "Operate!
We'll try to save her life." What life is it
if she can't think?—humiliation of
poor flesh, gasping its dumb dependency!

    You cut her open and her soul flew out,
leaving a limp creation, an imposter.

I watch you lift your glass, and I can see
my daughter in your hands, numbering
her ribs beneath the skin, naming the organs:
liver, colon, lungs and spleen. How could
your fingers know if she is lying there?
Touching like that's no cure for loneliness—
that's why I left my wife, and why I want
my daughter cherished more than hands can do.

    When Margaret was thirteen, we visited
the lake we lived by when she was a child.
Explaining why I had abandoned home,
I said "Mother and I have fallen out
of touch." We don't touch when our bodies touch
was what I couldn't bring myself to say.
She hugged me as the spindrift loon-calls spread
across the water with the evening mist;
then she pulled back. Softly as possible,
I put my arm around her as we walked,
and yet my love could not reach far enough
inside where love gets recognized as love.

    Then there was nothing I could do except
protect her from my own possessiveness,
and now I must protect her happiness
from you. Maybe I'm wrong, so here's a test
to prove you too can honor suffering:
doctors have professional ways of easing
people out of pain. Release my mother
from the dungeon of her bones; give her a pill
to rescue her. Margaret need never know;
I won't breathe one small sound of what we've said,
but I'll know that you're capable of love.
You'll have a father's blessing if you do.

TRYING TO SEPARATE

Please give me room, Howard! I've tried before
to tell you this—I have to leave you, oh
that came out wrong, there's no way I can find
the words that sound as if I'm making sense.
Not you, Howard, it isn't you I'm leaving,
it's Vermont, the starving deer, the spring
that never comes, the gloomy ice and clay.
Even when late sun lingers in the birches,
darkness fills my mind. I need more light,
more red—not just a pair of cardinals,
but flocks of them. There's no red in the earth;
purple spreads in the mountains when the sun
descends behind the hemlock trees as if
the animals were grieving there. And fall
comes much too soon, the yellows are too brief;
I don't have time here to forget myself.

I want to go to Tucson where I lived
before my mother died, where stones are red,
the desert light feels red—a gradual,
slow, steady red. I need more time to dwell
on images I want to paint. Don't joke
again about my always seeing red!
You once said that my painting is the cause,
but that's not first; I need a different light
than you to see, and then the paintings come.
You need Vermont, you need an inward light;
you need the feeling that each day is hard.

Love cannot feed itself with love. We've tried.
Love needs something outside itself—children—
and we've delayed deciding that too long.
You said one only chooses children after
one has had them; then they become like place,
then they're the given like the landscape is.

You think there's got to be some deeper cause
for breaking up. I fear you may be right,
but I can't find that cause; Howard, believe me,
I've really looked. All that I know is red,
and you desire gray; punishing winter
is your season, white birches are your light.
You need Vermont to be yourself. You do!
        Don't try to comfort me; don't touch me now—
that makes me angry when I want to talk—
for then you'll have a reason I should stay.
You'll say: admit it's me you want to leave,
admit you're angry, that it's not because
you love the goddamn red; you'll say we have our sunsets
blazing on the snow, we have our fire at night,
as if I'll give in like I always do.

TRYING TO RECONCILE

You shouldn't have gone off the pill without
your telling me! Even if we decide
 to have the child now, even if it's mine,
it was your choice, so don't pretend your motive
was to help our marriage last. A prick
groping in the dark for some anonymous
relief, that's all you wanted me to be,
that's all I am. If you believe a child
can bind our lives, allow me time to come
to feel that for myself. But it's control
you want—another way I'll need you and
you've got me then! I want a child to free
something in me more generous than sex
that brings me back to my own emptiness.
I've got to reach you, and I've got to try
to try, or else I'm only me again.
        Maybe we've lived in this same house too long.
I see the same striations in the cliffs
emerging orange from the mist each dawn.
The short-eared owl—I've seen him sitting like
a glacier in the moonlit apple tree
a hundred times, the same ancestral grip
still holding him, the mouse limp in his beak,
always the victim with his testament
of blood upon the snow in March, and yet
without regret like you and me, breathing
our remorseful sleep, blaming each other
for what we lack ourselves. Maybe we need
enemies to injure, more loves to betray,
to learn those cosmic patterns of defeat—
like limestone fossils in our hearth. I could
read pity there if we asked less of love
to rescue us from being what we are.

Watching the stars, pity is what I feel
for all of us, groping with thoughts of leaving
our own lives, banished even from ourselves
like stars receding with their reddened speed.
Will they come hurtling back, explode, and start
the whole damned thing again? I'll rant my way
back to my life—at least that's better than
accusing you of my own emptiness.

   It torments me to watch the whipping snow
piling against the trees to starve the deer
who die without a plea in their white minds
for help to come. "Hidden death" you called the pill,
"refusing to accept we'll be replaced."
It's like my fantasy of strangling you—
as if to take a life could save my own.

   Look there by the gully—it's the lame fox
whose broken leg we set last summer when
he was abandoned as a cub, staring
at us with his black eyes. Is there a chance
that he remembers us? "An empty casket
where a life should be," those were your words
that made me taste the murder in the pill.

   "Someone has got to help that wounded fox,"
you said, "since its own mother won't." "That's not
the way that Nature works," was my reply;
"now she's forgotten it's alive." You know
I'll love the child. You know I know it's mine,
don't you? I have no choice except to choose—
choose something or we're all just whirling dust,
just snow blind wind heaps on the blinding snow.

MAKING BELIEVE

I know it's not the first time you've been stung.
I know it hurt; the swelling closed your eye.
When I was stung I threw up from the shock.
But I can't sell our hives. Sweetheart, caring
for our bees, raising them with Jim's help, makes
me feel the seasons turn. If I believed
in God, "I'll tilt the planet" would be His
initial words. Jim's almost old enough
to tend the hives himself; when he removes
the honey all the watching bees stay calm—
as if they trusted him. When honey bees
are shipped, the queen bee is protected in
her own small wooden box, surrounded by
thousands of worker bees. If she were not
secluded in her cage the other bees
would kill her, since the odor she emits
would overwhelm their tuned intelligence.
    And so a sugar cube is fitted in
a hole on one side of her cage. After
we shake the bees into their hive—I've let
Jim handle them for years—the boxed-in queen
is lowered down to them. The time they take
to eat the cube and thus release the queen
into the colony, allows them to
adjust themselves to her so she can move
toward darkness at the bottom of the hive
where she will lay her eggs. The colony
is like a tree—a single living thing
with separate parts: roots, trunk, flowers, and leaves.
    The worker bees collect the food—like leaves
from sunlit air; the queen, like roots and trunk,
connects one generation to the next;
born in the spring, drones resemble flowers

in their brief flourishing. The queen retains
their genitals after they mate and die;
death is no tragedy to them. Their lives
continue in the colony as if
their whole philosophy might read: "The bees
that follow me are who I am." When Jim
and I last gathered honey from the hive,
the sweetness so excited him that he
forgot he wore his black protecting veil
and wildly threw his arms around my neck.

    I'll tell you something bees can't do; they can't
pretend. Imagine you are me, wishing
to will your son a gift just like the trust
a nursing infant's body learns upon
his mother's breast. Think of me feeling that!
For him the morning light is still blue shadows
hazing into purple shades; besides
his mother's breath, he hears the knocking of
a bee against a window where a vase
contains a sprig of cherry blooms. Sweetness
is what we need to be remembered by.

    After two years, when the fatigued queen bee's
fertility diminishes, she is
deposed by worker bees. But that's where all
analogies collapse. We need to make
believe that human love has lasting seasons
of its own—as we once vowed to do.

    Don't try to pluck the stinger out! Some honey
smeared upon the swollen flesh will help
as well as any remedy I know.

MAKING HER WILL

Since Tom was born, I've never flown with you;
if we crash now, my brother and his wife
should be the children's guardians. She cares—
her table always has a bowl of fruit;
the pans above her stove make a design
of rising circles like the sun at dawn.
And when Stan built the wall around their house
with stones that he and Donny gathered from
the river bed, he would call "Now!" and swoosh,
from Donny's hands to his, the stone would slide
in place as if the mortared wall had willed
itself. I watched them work before you said
you wanted children of your own; your voice
was so deliberate you frightened me.

How could you let your sister raise our boys?
Painting is what she loves—in her queer way:
her morning valley mists are purple; even
her pines and hemlocks have a purple hue;
her still-lifes have no peaches, only plums
and shadows of more plums. Don't laugh as if
I mean this merely as a joke! Your sister
has a purple soul; she thinks she'll live
forever in some paradise of angels
lounging in their purple clouds. And if
she can't face death, how can she raise a child?
Paintings may last, but they don't live or die.
Maybe this summer at the waterfall
a child will drown just as your brother did.
A dead child is more loss than any mind
can hold; like mountains hazing into dusk;
like purple dusk dissolving into night.

Don't watch me from the corners of your eyes.
That's what your sister does. Her portrait of you
caught the rigid way you tilt your head—

as if your brother's voice called from beyond
the painting's edge. White tinted hair, she put
her white gloves on and stood there with her hand
poised in the surgical, fluorescent light,
glaring at her blank canvas till your lips
emerged an oily wet, with purple curves.
And then, for ornament, she made those curves
again, sketching your eyebrows and your ears.
Those curves were what she cared about—they made
her smile! I saw it sweep across her face!
I swear, if heaven is just, she'll have to scrub
the angels' underwear a hundred years
before her penance is complete. For what?
For purple curves—not loving life enough
to grieve we circle back into the dark.

      Your sister paints in order to forget
that nothing lasts; because your brother died,
she can't be faithful to a living man.
How can she raise a child? You are like her;
your brother's death is still locked up in you
as if you could decide to keep him there
alive by holding back against your grief.

      Did you decide to fall in love with me?
Maybe your sorrow did, to free itself;
you need my tears to weep your own. I see
the mountain, you, our gentle, handsome boys—
everything I love—hazing into dusk;
I picture it as if it's taken place—
that's why I am afraid to fly today.

      I've got to win this argument because—
because my brother and his son together
built a wall around their house; because
my brother's wife keeps peaches in a bowl!
You could decide, my love, and willingly
so that you'll be a model for our sons,
to let my passion have its purple way.

I hear the phoebe; she's returned to her
same nest this year. Are you awake? I smell
crab apple blossoms lifting on the wind;
they must be opening. Throughout the night,
perhaps the soft vibrating of the stars—
something kept startling me, as if I had
good news to tell you, but I can't think what
it is. We've lived together fifty years,
our lives are what they were. How long is it
since we've made love?—there, now, at last it's said,
it's openly between us, though we've shared
the knowledge every time we've almost touched.
Like fifty years ago, before we first
made love, old age makes you forbidden now.

    I picture you on Grandpa's farm, sitting
beside a stream, watching the maple leaves,
yellow and red, riding the blazing foam.
My brother, with a sailboat on a string,
played on the other shore, and so I paused,
uncertain—should I try to kiss you now?
A sweat-drop blew across your cheek and left
a hieroglyph as if on sun-warmed stone.
I must have held the kiss too long, because
you drew back. "No, not now," your breathing whispered.

    On the first night that you nursed Paul at home,
I watched the lamp behind you make a line
of hazy light to shape your silhouette.
I'd never seen your features quite so still;
you looked like Grandma on her cameo.
I laid my head upon your arm; "Not now,"
you said, "I don't think it will snow tonight."
I didn't ask if "Not now" was a sentence
meant for me, or for the coming snow.

    Last night you called out in your sleep, and then

I dreamed you visited my mother's house;
you both were standing at the open door,
she in a purple, flowered dress, and you
in white with noon sun reddening your hair.
You argued, though I couldn't hear the words;
she blocked your way from getting in the house.
I watched, and from the attic window where
I knelt upon a box, thinking I was
a child, I saw my hands upon the sill,
swollen with old, blue veins. A man came out,
with no shirt on, palms covering his face,
his skin white where the fingertips pressed in,
his shadowed muscles flowing down his arms;
you took his hand and started off with him.
"Don't go," I shouted, "Please don't go!" He turned,
lowered his hands, and gazed back in the house.
          The young man there—that's who I was, that's who
you left me for! He paused once more, and then
you walked together down a pathway toward
a windless lake, diminishing within
an arching row of willow trees. We're told
that's how we see the farthest galaxies,
receding almost at the speed of light,
and vanishing except for their "red shift."
So what we know is only where they've left from
empty millions of light-years ago.
          News of the past arriving in the night:
your hair in sunlight and your silhouette;
the phoebe's whistle, and the thick odor
of blossoms opening; wet wind settling
and merging with the soft hiss of the snow;
everything held still in the mind at once,
everything here, and lost, and being lost,
equally unfolding, equally gone.
The autumn berries of the ash tree glimmer
orange in the January snow,

as evening darkens, shifting into red.
    Before the cedar waxwings left our house,
they could not eat them all; some are still here,
shrunken and brown, still clinging to the tree.
And you are here, and what we were—is here;
news of the past, I smell it in the dawn.
I feel that if I tried to love you now,
I'd gather in your breath, and hold it in
my own, and speak red, youthful words again.

PRAYER FOR PRAYER

Darling, splitting the wood can wait until
the wind dies down. I want to try to say
what's troubling me, although we vowed before
we married that we'd keep our own beliefs
and let the children choose. They've left home now;
there's not much more that we can do for them;
it's you and me together, only us,
and I'm afraid you won't get into heaven,
not having turned to God. Without you, how
could I be happy there, unless God wills
that I forget this life? I don't want that!
The March sun hasn't thawed those icicles
gleaming along the edges of our roof;
perhaps this constant wind has numbed my faith.
    I've never had to ask you this before,
but would you try to pray? Make up the words
if only for my sake; start thanking God
for daily things like breakfast oranges
heaped in the yellow bowl your mother painted—
a couple bathing in a waterfall—
our wedding gift of thirty years ago;
thank Him for your routine: feeding the birds
in winter, pruning apple trees in spring;
thank Him for splitting wood. You know I know
that even when you grumble, still it's work
you love. Nothing I do will feel complete
until I've given thanks for doing it,
so that I'm not alone: like thanking you
for thanking me when I prepare a meal
adds grace to grace. That's not a phrase you'd use;
you would prefer to hold some meanings back:
"Grace is not fattening, how can it hurt?"
but what we feel is not so far apart,

though maybe it's the very space God wants
to test us with? My mother used to say:
"You cannot cling to what you love with all
your strength; God made some special part of us
for letting go." I understood her when
our children left, and I can almost see
the spaces where they were. Maybe sorrow
is allowed in heaven, so God won't have to
cancel human love by making us forget?

     I won't forget, not willingly; one day
in paradise, watching the clouds, I'd think
of you standing beside the frozen stream,
eyeing the wood still to be split and stacked,
and I'd be back on earth—at least at heart.
God means for marriages to end with death,
but after that the Bible isn't clear.
Perhaps God's love begins where human love
completes itself, and yet I'll never tire
of the past we've shared. I know you'll promise me
you'll try to pray, and then you'll ask the Lord
to help me find the strength to give up prayer—
as if God would enjoy your joke; you'll swear:
"By yonder icicle, I'll love the world
until it does me in!" Thought hurts the most;
we can't escape the sorrow of an end
without an end, death going on and on.
Although you never speak of it, I know
your father died while he was splitting wood;
your mother's telling always starts the same:
"Some snow had fallen on his knitted hat . . . "
as if for her all time had stopped. Maybe
that is what heaven's like? She seems to smile,
but then the age lines darken in her face.

     Darling, I know you know something in me
approves your laughing at my need to pray.
By yonder icicle, what human love

allows, we have! But don't stand grinning with
that orange in your mouth as if you were
some sacrificial pig! Go split more wood
while I put dinner on; listen to God's
silences even as the wind blows through
the icicles and piles snow by our shed;
we may be in for quite a night of it.

AUTHOR'S EPILOGUE

Go little book, get the hell out of here,
I've had enough of these imagined lives
invented to augment my finite own.
I want at last to be a character
distinct, believable in my own right,
content in authoring myself, although,
Lord knows, my story needs embellishing,
so incoherent as it is, without
a unifying theme, except perhaps
for my ongoing love for lakes and trees,
my wife, my children, and my friends, my dog
now barking up some mythic tree—the one
perhaps where Sigmund got his phallic sword,
my three-legged cat, "Survivor," and his son,
"Survivor II," who also has used up
his randy lives, their names a catalyst
(Hail, Muse, of doubly resonating puns!)
to memory. And yet, dear reader, all
you know of me is what's narrated here,
so how can you surmise I have a life
other than what these words convey—a life
on which these improvising words depend?
    Try visualizing me with a trimmed beard,
now mainly white, my eyes a little teary
from the wind, sitting in my carved chair
and watching as the evening light flares out
across the snow-tipped mountain peaks—
a vista so impersonal it helps
me to condense my life and turn myself
into a character—just one among
the others I've recorded here. Although
I've never pulled a sword out of a tree,
my questing blood has been augmented by

that great Wagnerian orchestral flow
bestowing grandeur on my base desires.
       I've kept a vigilance, as best I could,
in my authentic ebbing life, on those
within the circle of my widened care,
though there are sorrows even kindness lacks
the power to mitigate, and that is true
of all the stories that I've tried to tell.
       Yet there are times when laughter set me free,
transcending suffering and loss, as when
two tipsy atoms walked into a bar
and one, while weeping in his beer, proclaimed
"I've lost my one electron." "Are you sure?"
his sympathetic brother queried him.
"I'm positive," was his reply. This too,
dear reader, is a tale of loss transformed
to affirmation if you've summoned holy
empathy enough to care about
a person's struggle with identity,
down to the molecules of which we're made.
       And now add music, Maestro, to the mix
(My Muse has always been androgynous
as the conception of this stressed book shows) —
music whose power to be beautiful
when sad, allows one momentarily
to feel triumphant over death itself,
whereby I'm free to grant my characters,
including me myself, the grace to be
themselves alone, complete and permanent,
composed in their own atmosphere as when
I'm walking by a lake among hushed trees,
the purple mountain peaks reflected in
the languid water's multiplying light
with all the swelling music of farewell,
distilled from laughter, on my worded lips,

resolved with the conviction that it's time
to vanish into silence with a rhyme.